FOLLOW
MY
LEAD

HarperCollins*Publishers*
1 London Bridge Street
London SE1 9GF

www.harpercollins.co.uk

HarperCollins*Publishers*
Macken House, 39/40 Mayor Street Upper
Dublin 1, D01 C9W8, Ireland

First published by HarperCollins*Publishers* 2025

1 3 5 7 9 10 8 6 4 2

A catalogue record of this book is available from the British Library

ISBN 978-0-00-872067-4

Printed and bound by GPS Group in Bosnia and Herzegovina

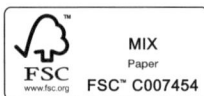

FOLLOW MY LEAD

UK WALKING ADVENTURES FOR YOU AND YOUR DOG

EMILY GILL

HarperCollins*Publishers*

Contents

INTRODUCTION   6

EAST OF ENGLAND
1. WELLS-NEXT-THE-SEA   11
2. BURNHAM MARKET   17
3. CAMBRIDGE   23
4. WROXHAM   31
5. SOUTHWOLD   37
6. HOLT   43

MIDLANDS
7. BAKEWELL   53
8. STRATFORD-UPON-AVON   61
9. BUXTON   67

NORTH WEST
10. KESWICK   77
11. GRASMERE   85
12. MANCHESTER   91

NORTH EAST
13. CRASTER   99
14. TYNEMOUTH   105
15. BAMBURGH   113

YORKSHIRE
16. YORK   121
17. ROBIN HOOD'S BAY   127
18. HARROGATE   133

SCOTLAND

19. EDINBURGH   143
20. ISLE OF ARRAN   149
21. INVERNESS   155

WALES

22. BARMOUTH   165
23. TENBY   171
24. ANGLESEY   179

SOUTH EAST

25. BATTERSEA   187
26. BRIGHTON   193
27. ISLE OF WIGHT   201

COTSWOLDS

28. BOURTON-ON-THE-WATER   211
29. BURFORD   217
30. BROADWAY   225

SOUTH WEST

31. DARTMOUTH   235
32. LULWORTH COVE   243
33. WELLS   251
34. ROCK   259
35. WOOLACOMBE   265

PICTURE CREDITS   272

Introduction

It's easy to take it for granted, but the UK is home to some of the most stunning scenery in the world. From breathtaking coastal paths and beautiful beaches to historic city jaunts and charming countryside – we're so lucky to be home to so many amazing places.

And the best part about exploring the UK? Your dog can come too. If you're like me, no trip is complete without your four-legged friend by your side! Exploring with our dogs can be incredibly fulfilling and enjoyable, offering so many benefits to both mental and physical health; helping us to slow down, be more mindful, and get away from the rat race of day-to-day life.

Making the most of the time we have with our dogs to make memories is something I'm truly passionate about. It's why I set up my social media pages @greatbritishdogwalks where I share my favourite dog-friendly places to visit and explore. The UK is one of the most dog-friendly countries in the world and there is so much to experience.

However, I know it can be difficult to know where to start, and to figure out whether somewhere is truly 'dog friendly'. So that's where this book comes in. In these pages you will find 35 locations across the UK, all of which are great bases for some amazing walks and adventures.

At each location, I have highlighted some key dog-friendly hotspots, as well as where to stay, where to enjoy a bite to eat and drink, the best dog-friendly activities, and even the wildlife you might see along the way. I hope this book inspires you and your dog to explore both what's on your doorstep and the best the UK has to offer.

BEFORE YOU GET STARTED: TRAVEL TIPS FOR YOU AND YOUR DOG

From the rolling hills of the Cotswolds to the rugged coastline of Northumberland, the UK offers countless walking routes perfect for dogs, but it is important to follow a few guidelines to help make your trip stress-free.

- Always research the area before you go. Look into whether the walk is suitable for your dog, and consider whether they are fit enough for the terrain.
- Pay attention to any seasonal restrictions – particularly when visiting beaches or nature reserves.
- Be mindful of the weather and your dog's condition. The UK's weather can be unpredictable, so be prepared for rain and mud, or heatwaves in the summer months.
- Packing the essentials is also key: fresh water, a portable dog water bowl, treats and poo bags are a must.
- Keep your dog on a lead when walking along cliff paths or beside fast-flowing rivers.

The Countryside Code is a set of guidelines that help protect nature and farmland, whilst also ensuring everyone – humans and animals alike – can enjoy the outdoors safely. One of the most important rules when walking with your dog is to always keep them under control. If you're walking near livestock or wildlife, keep your dog on a lead, and if you pass through a gate, leave it as you find it.

Another crucial point is to always pick up after your dog. Not only is this courteous to other walkers, but dog waste can also be harmful to the environment. Be sure to dispose of it properly, too.

By following these tips and respecting the Countryside Code, you and your dog can enjoy the beauty of the UK's landscapes while ensuring they remain preserved and welcoming for everyone to explore in the future.

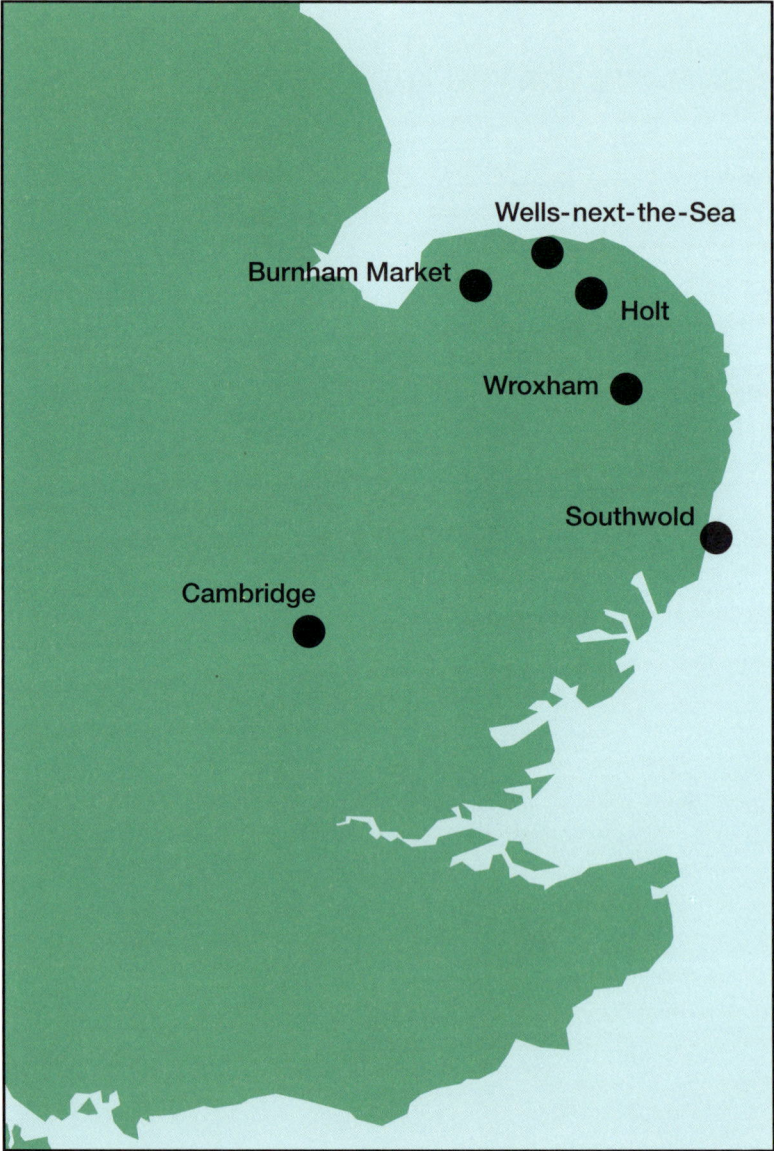

Wells-next-the-Sea

Burnham Market

Holt

Wroxham

Southwold

Cambridge

East of England

Wells-next-the-Sea	11
Burnham Market	17
Cambridge	23
Wroxham	31
Southwold	37
Holt	43

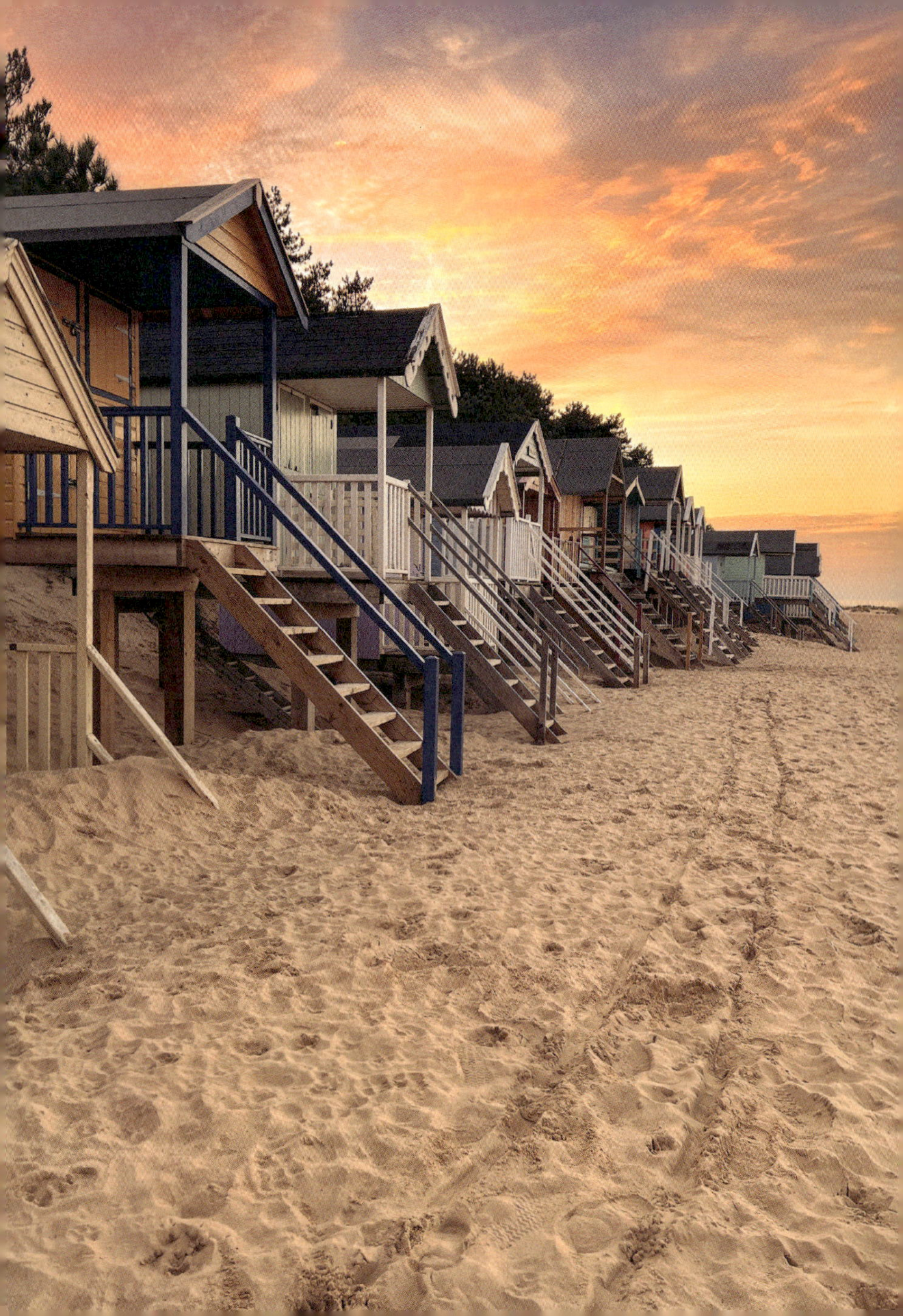

1.

Wells-next-the-Sea

North Norfolk, for me, just epitomises doggy heaven – it has miles of unspoilt, sandy (and most importantly dog-friendly year-round) beaches to explore. At the heart of the coast is Wells-next-the-Sea, a bustling seaside town, which is perfect for all the family.

The sweeping golden sandy beach is bordered by beautiful pinewoods and colourful beach huts. At low tide, the sands here stretch for miles, and as it's part of the North Norfolk Coast Path and Peddars Way, you and your dog can walk for as long as you like.

The brightly decorated beach huts at Wells are instantly recognisable, stood on stilts at the back of the sand with stunning views of the beach, and set against the backdrop of Corsican pines. You can even hire one for the day – a great dog-friendly experience that I'd highly recommend. They are the perfect place for your dog to cool off on a hot summer's day, or to shelter from the elements if it's a windy or wet one. Plus, what's better than a freshly brewed cuppa on the beach?

You might get the chance to spot some rare birds here, including oystercatchers, terns and avocets, and if you're really lucky, you'll see common and grey seals too. Dog-friendly seal boat trips are available for those wanting to enjoy all that this part of the coastline has to offer.

A mile from the beach is Wells-next-the-Sea harbour, where you'll often see children crabbing on the quay and people enjoying the finest fish and chips the UK has to offer while watching the fishing boats come and go.

Walk a little further and you'll amble down Staithe Street, a high street where a mix of traditional and contemporary shops can be found – many of which are dog friendly. In fact, if you don't have a dog here, you're sure to look out of place.

In the heart of Wells lies The Buttlands, a leafy green Georgian square, which is flanked by some great dog-friendly pubs, one of my favourites being The Globe Inn. It's the perfect place to enjoy a delicious meal, a truly warm welcome, and when there is good sunny weather, you can make use of its fantastic beer garden.

While holidaying here you wouldn't get bored if you stayed within the confines of Wells-next-the-Sea itself, but it also makes a great base, with some amazing beaches and things to do just a very short distance away.

Places to explore

HOLKHAM BEACH

Lady Anne's Drive, Holkham, NR23 1RG

Starting at Lady Anne's Drive, walk down the boardwalk and eventually you'll arrive at Holkham Beach – one of the most unspoilt stretches of sand in the country, and often referred to as the 'jewel of the North Norfolk Coast' – and it's easy to see why. There are sometimes dog restrictions due to the nesting ground birds here, but 70 per cent of the beach is still free for off-lead zoomies all year round.

If you walk a little further up, you eventually come to Holkham Hall, a gorgeous eighteenth-century country house, surrounded by rolling parkland and herds of fallow deer. It's particularly great here for kids, with a fantastic adventure playground, and has plenty for adults to explore too, including a traditional walled garden and picture-perfect boating lake.

WELLS-NEXT-THE-SEA BEACH HUTS

Probably one of the most recognisable things about Wells-next-the-Sea is the traditional beach huts that flank the white sands. Hiring one for the day provides a great base, particularly on wet or hot days.

BLAKENEY POINT

Home to England's largest grey seal colony and uninterrupted views of the North Norfolk coastline, Blakeney Point is a must-visit for nature buffs. There are some dog restrictions throughout the year, so make sure you check out the National Trust website, or alternatively, hop on one of the dog-friendly seal trips from Wells-next-the-Sea harbour.

Places to eat, drink and stay

PLATTEN'S FISH AND CHIPS
The Quay, NR23 1AH

Located right on the sea front, Platten's is a family run chippie that serves some of the best fish and chips in the UK. It's dog friendly inside, so you'll have the choice of eating in the warm or soaking up that sea breeze sat on the quay.

THE THREE HORSESHOES
69 The Street, Warham, NR23 1NL

A traditional English pub with real character in the small hamlet of Warham, The Three Horseshoes pub is home to one of the best roast dinners I've had in North Norfolk, and is also steeped in history, dating back to 1725.

PINEWOODS HOLIDAY PARK
Beach Road, NR23 1DR

Pinewoods Holiday Park offers a range of static caravans and luxury lodges alongside camping options and couldn't be better located for exploring the beach and surrounding woods. I return year after year.

THE GLOBE INN
The Buttlands, NR23 1EU

Overlooking the very pretty Buttland's square, The Globe Inn is located in the heart of the town, making for a hard-earned cold drink after a long walk, with a laid-back vibe. The food menu is extensive and also includes a doggy menu (always a plus in my book!)

All of the 19 cosy bedrooms are thoughtfully designed with your canine companion in mind, and come with their own dog bed, towel and water bowl.

THE VICTORIA
Park Road, Holkham, NR23 1RG

Perfectly situated just a stone's throw from Holkham Beach and Holkham Hall, The Victoria boasts a curated menu of locally sourced ingredients. The orangery is particularly beautiful, with light and airy views over the reserve. It's dog friendly throughout, and if you're into your food you'll definitely want to add this one to your tick list.

Alongside being a fantastic restaurant, The Victoria is also home to 10 dog-friendly rooms, each with their own distinct charm.

The Burnhams Tea Room & Cafe
The Burnhams Tea Room & Cafe
JOULES

2.

Burnham Market

Lying just 3 miles from the coast, Burnham Market is a seventeenth-century Norfolk village bursting with character.

Beautifully picturesque, the village is centred around a perfectly kept green, which is flanked by lots of independent shops and boutiques. In fact, it's pretty traditional here, with the high-street being home to a post office, butchers, hardware shop, fishmongers and chemist, alongside 30 independent shops selling everything from unique artwork and tasty deli treats to stylish clothing and books.

This is a place where you and your pup can escape the hustle and bustle of a city and soak up a traditional village atmosphere that oozes style. And you definitely won't go hungry here, as the village is home to a mix of renowned pubs and restaurants (please see some favourites listed overleaf).

Surrounded by smaller villages, it also makes a great starting point for many fantastic walks. I particularly love 'The Burnhams', a route that takes you round three of these, including Burnham Overy Staithe, once a thriving seaport.

Burnham Market is a fantastic location for exploring this area of coastline as it's nice and central. There are lots of things to do just a short drive or bus ride away and it's so well connected, being well served by the Coasthopper bus, which runs all the way to Hunstanton.

One of the standout places to visit is Drove Orchards, a popular rural market located a few miles up the coast, which has a range of shops, cafés and restaurants, including a pizza place in a yurt!

As it's only a mile from the glorious North Norfolk coast, you'll also be just a stone's throw from the beautiful dog-friendly beaches while in

Burnham Market. One of the best is Holme-next-the-Sea. Like many on this part of the English coast, it has sweeping golden sands and is backed by pines – although I'd say this one is somewhat of a hidden gem as very few people know about it. Even in the height of summer you can find you have the majority of the beach to yourselves.

Nearby you'll also find Brancaster Beach, another jewel a short drive from the village, known for long stretches of sand and shallow waters. Similarly to most of the beaches in the area, dogs are welcome here year-round, making it a great spot for a coastal walk.

Places to explore

BRANCASTER BEACH

Beach Road, Brancaster, PE31 8BW

A huge expanse of golden sand that seems to go on for miles, backed by beautiful natural dunes. Walk to the left as you look at the sea, and you'll eventually come to Titchwell Marsh, a RSPB reserve and haven for bird watchers. Make sure you check the tide times, as during a high Spring tide the car park can become flooded.

DROVE ORCHARDS

Thornham Road, Hunstanton, PE36 6LS

Around 15 minutes away from Burnham Market you'll find Drove Orchards, a popular rural market with a range of quirky shops, a café and some pretty cool dog-friendly eateries. If you've ever watched Gilmore Girls you'll know what I mean when I say this place really gives 'Stars Hollow' vibes.

HOLME-NEXT-THE-SEA NATURE RESERVE AND BEACH

Broadwater Road, Hunstanton, PE36 6LQ

One of the hidden gems of North Norfolk's coastline, Holme-next-the-Sea Nature Reserve is a peaceful and untouched wilderness where land, sea and sky meet. It's dog friendly year-round and a fantastic beach for a walk. Head back into the dunes and you'll stumble across the Norfolk Wildlife Trust's visitor centre and a great little café that even serves doggy ice cream.

Places to eat, drink and stay 🐾🐾

ERIC'S PIZZERIA
Drove Orchards, Thornham Road, PE36 6LS

Eric's Pizzeria is housed in a cosy circular yurt, making it quite the unique dining experience! The wood-fired pizza is fantastic, and well worth the short drive out of Burnham Market. They also offer takeaway options.

NO. TWENTY9
29 Market Place, PE31 8HF

The rooms at No. Twenty9 are nestled in their own peaceful garden and have a sense of tranquillity about them – it would make the perfect romantic stay! Each of the rooms are beautifully decorated, have their own patio area with outside seating (perfect for dogs) and some even have a free-standing bath.

DEEPDALE CAMPING AND ROOMS
Deepdale Granary, Main Road, PE31 8DD

If luxury isn't your dog's thing, Deepdale Camping and Rooms is a quiet, award-winning and eco-friendly campsite in the village of Burnham Deepdale (just over 2 miles away from Burnham Market). They also have a range of private rooms if you're looking for a cheaper option.

THE WHITE HORSE
Main Road, Brancaster Staithe, PE31 8BY

Located just down the road in Brancaster Staithe, The White Horse is situated overlooking the stunning marshland. They have an amazing seafood menu, and the sunset views from their terrace are not to be missed. In the summer they even open up a bar Marshside, with its own special menu – the perfect spot to enjoy the sunshine and soak up the atmosphere.

THE HOSTE ARMS
The Green, PE31 8HD

At the heart of the village lies The Hoste Arms. Inside you'll find a traditional bar steeped in history with a lovely welcoming log burner to warm your cockles on a cold day. The food here is locally sourced and they even have locally brewed beer too.

The Hoste Arms also offers dog-friendly rooms. If you're looking for something boujee, this is the perfect place to stay, with a private cinema room, a gym and a luxury on-site spa. A few of the rooms also have a private terrace.

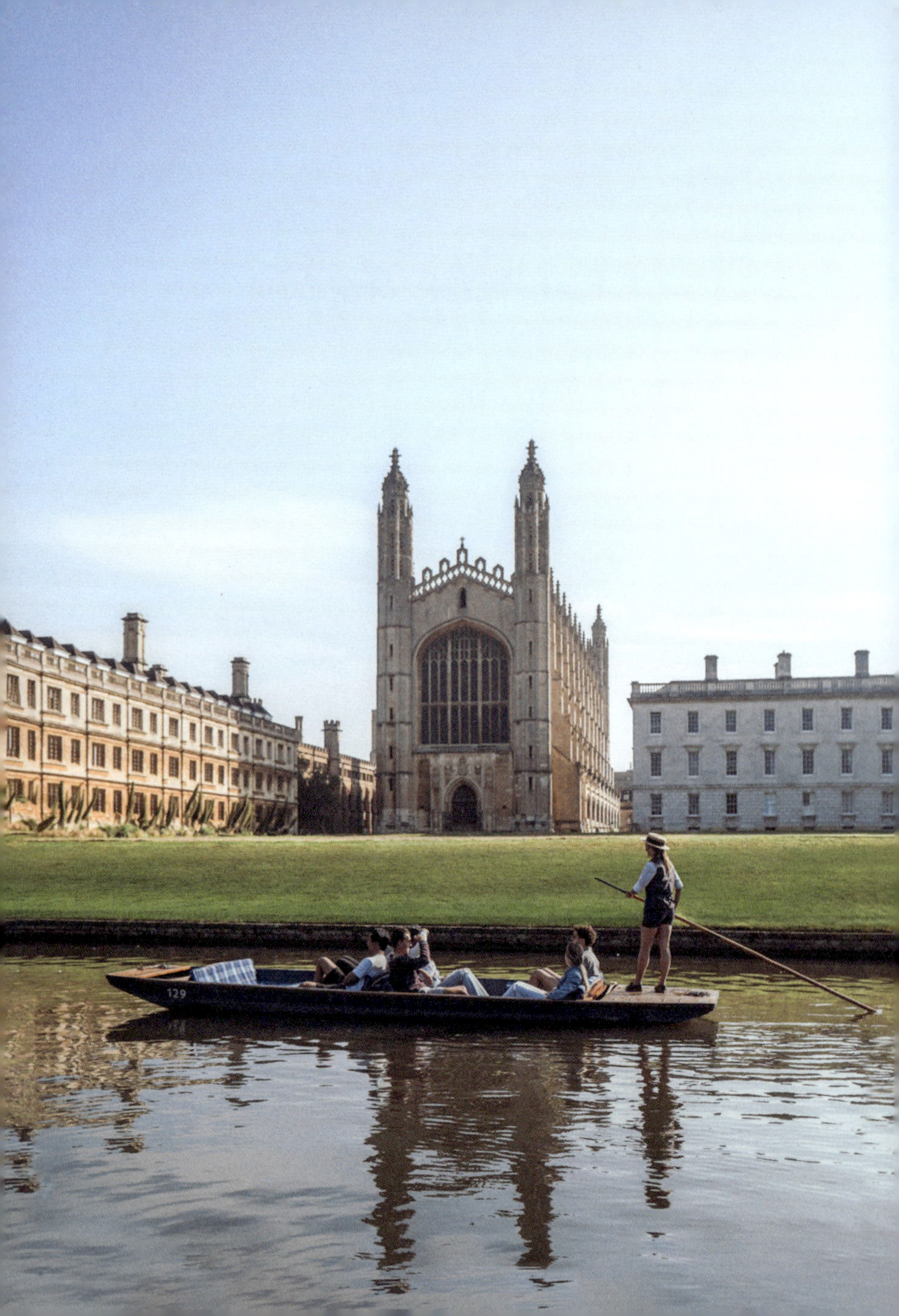
129

3.

Cambridge

Famous for its world-renowned university, Cambridge is a hub for innovation and creativity, steeped in history and some pretty inspiring architecture.

Cambridge exudes a magical charm that feels almost timeless. It has a grandeur and allure that is perfectly paired with quaint cobbled streets. It's incredibly scenic, making the perfect photo backdrop for any doggy portraits you wish to take.

You'll be able to wander the streets, exploring plenty of shops, pubs, bars and restaurants, and there is no shortage of green spaces either, with a range of walking routes you can take straight from the city centre across beautiful rural fields.

And of course, there are so many historical points of interest, a lot of them being outdoors, meaning you can have a fantastic day of sightseeing without having to leave your dog out. If you fancy learning a little more on your way around the city, you can even head out on a dog-friendly walking tour and be guided by an expert, or for the ultimate Cambridge experience, why not try punting on the River Cam? Most punts are dog friendly and allow you to take in some of Cambridge's most epic scenery at a leisurely pace.

The Cambridge Museum of Technology is another fantastic dog-friendly option. It guides you through the city's industrial heritage and also has a range of interesting exhibitions. Dogs are allowed throughout the museum as long as they are on a lead.

One of the best parts of Cambridge though is the abundance of green spaces, parks and walking routes. Milton Country Park is a favourite of mine, with miles of accessible paths to explore. There are also events throughout the year, with food stalls and a vintage bar in the summer.

Another great route is heading along the River Cam, starting from the heart of the city and leading towards Grantchester – a picturesque village known for its meadows, quaint tea rooms, and idyllic riverside picnic spots with serene views of the river and grazing cattle.

The train links are also fantastic here, meaning you'll be able to travel directly or with minimal changes from much of the UK, making this a great destination if you don't drive.

A short train ride away is Ely. Known for being 'quintessentially British', Ely is the second smallest city in England being home to an amazing cathedral that rises from the surrounding flat fenlands with a towering Gothic spire that can be seen for miles. You'll be able to explore the city's medieval streets here and take some of the fantastic walks along the River Great Ouse, which meanders past scenic meadows.

Places to explore

PUNTING TRIP

Scudamore's Punting Company, 32a Bridge Street, CB2 1UJ

Punting is absolutely top of my list of recommendations for Cambridge. Scudamore's punts allow dogs to join you and provide interesting information about the buildings you pass, including the King's College Chapel, the Wren Library, the Mathematical Bridge and the famous Bridge of Sighs.

CAMBRIDGE MUSEUM OF TECHNOLOGY

The Old Pumping Station, CB5 8LD

Often referred to as one of the country's leading hubs of technical innovation, Cambridge has bags of technological history. The Museum of Technology takes you through the industrial revolution to the present day and is a fantastic and inspiring day out. Dogs are welcome throughout on leads.

MILTON COUNTRY PARK

Cambridge Road, Milton, CB24 6AZ

Just north of Cambridge itself, Milton Country Park is home to 95 acres of parkland making it a great place to explore. You'll find plenty to do here beyond walking, including paddle sports, open water swimming, a playground and even a free orienteering course.

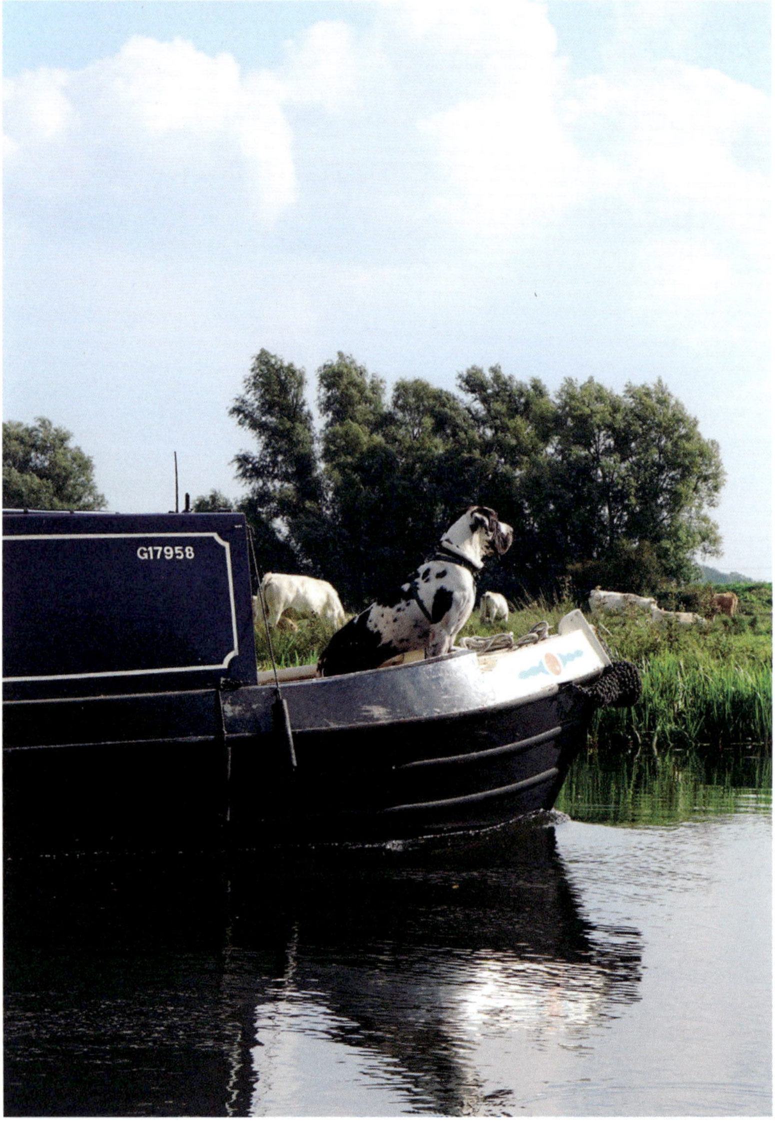
G17958

Places to eat, drink and stay 🐾🐾

HOT NUMBERS
4 Trumpington Street, CB2 1QA

Hot Numbers has a modern hygge style décor where you can grab a cup of coffee specially brewed at their own roastery. There is a laid-back vibe with an academic buzz, and a beautiful garden that provides the perfect suntrap.

PINT SHOP
10 Peas Hill, CB2 3PN

If craft beer is your thing, this one is for you. Pint shop is a contemporary bar with beers from both the UK and the rest of Europe, and a highly recommended dining menu and bar menu – both equally as delicious!

THE GONVILLE HOTEL
2 Gonville Place, CB1 1LY

The Gonville is one of those places that doesn't just welcome dogs, but adores them, with staff that will offer an abundance of fuss to four-legged friends, and even their very own welcome pack. For humans you can expect a luxuriously indulgent hotel, which would be perfect for a special getaway.

THE GRADUATE HOTEL
Granta Place, Mill Lane, CB2 1RT

Whenever I've asked my followers where they would recommend staying in Cambridge, this place has always come out top. It's a unique boutique hotel with rooms inspired by local history and university icons. At the heart of it all there's also a fantastic bar.

THE WATERMAN
32 Chesterton Road, CB4 3AX

A chic dog-friendly pub with comfortable rooms and very friendly staff, The Waterman has only eight rooms, and is great value for money. With tasteful décor the rooms are spacious and make for a great base when exploring the city.

THE OLD BICYCLE SHOP
104 Regent Street, CB2 1DP

The oldest bicycle shop in the country, Charles Darwin is even said to have bought a bike from this very shop in the 1800s! Now a quirky bar and restaurant, they are open for brunch, lunch and dinner alongside an extensive wine menu, and have plenty of vegan and veggie options too.

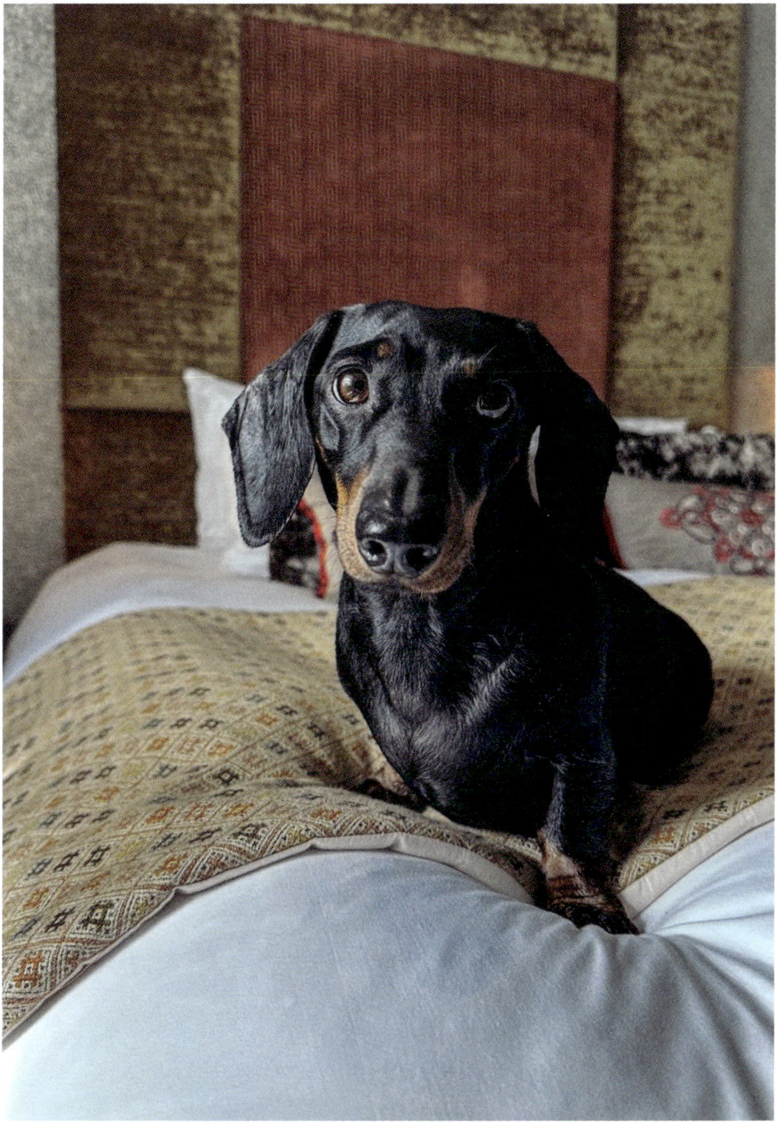

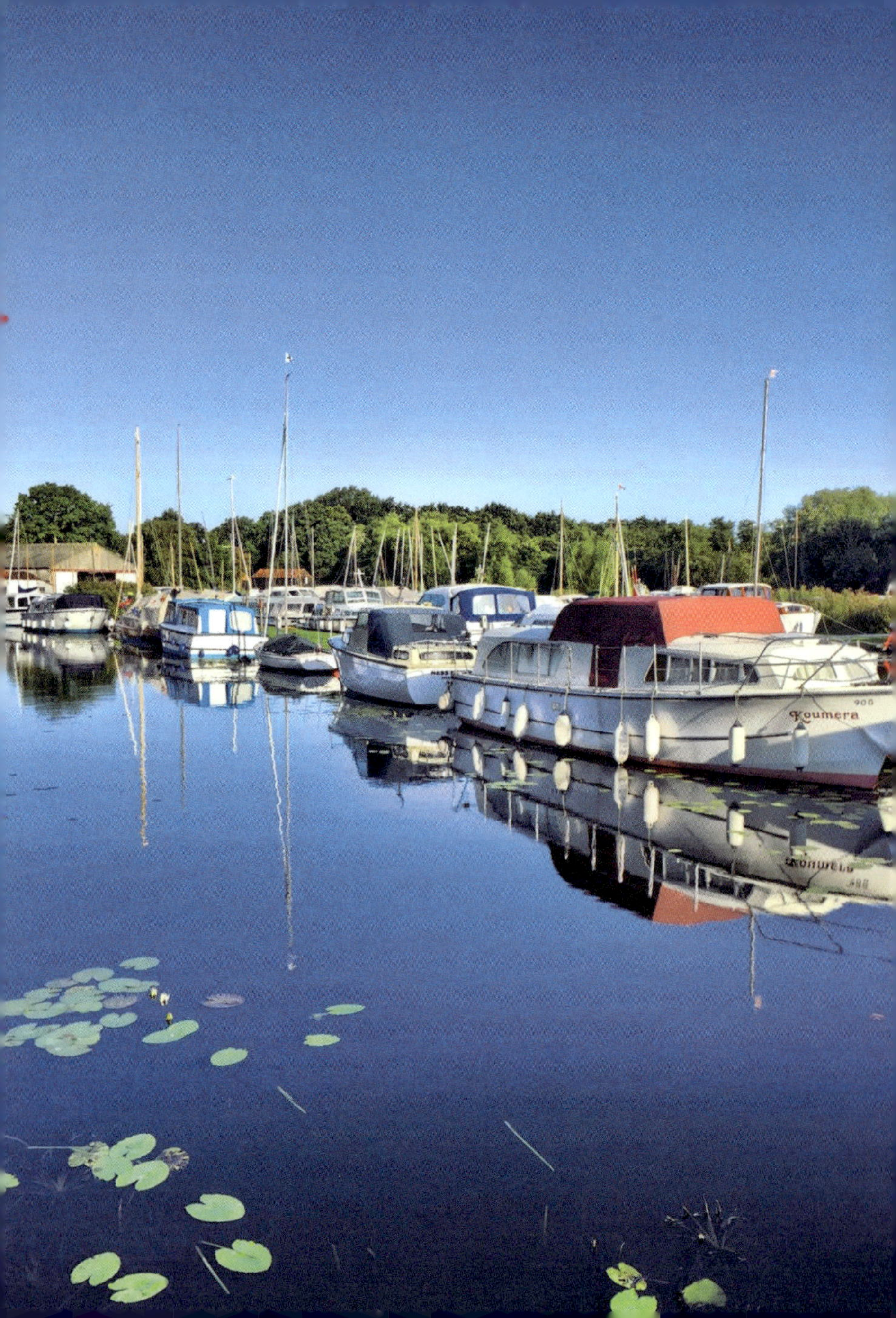
908
Koumera

4.

Wroxham

With over 190 miles of scenic footpaths to explore and countless picture-perfect views, the Norfolk Broads is an ideal destination for a dog-friendly getaway and is one of the UK's 15 national parks. Nestled in the heart of this breathtaking landscape, Wroxham, often known as the 'Capital of the Broads', offers the perfect starting point to immerse yourself in the area's natural beauty.

The best part, however, is the tranquil waterways, and it's the perfect destination for a boat trip. There are plenty you can hire for a few hours, the day or even to stay overnight on, which makes for a fantastic dog-friendly holiday with a difference.

Situated only 8 miles away from Norwich, you'll find plenty to do here, from walks exploring the waterways, to dog-friendly beaches like Waxham and Winterton just a short drive away. Lots of these beaches are dog friendly year-round, and unlike their North Norfolk counterparts tend to be a lot less busy, even in high season.

Inland, the River Bure runs through the heart of Wroxham and is a great place to go for a walk with beautiful scenery, and plenty of eateries and pubs to stop off at en route. There are also a variety of designated footpaths (over 190 miles) with several long-distance routes running through the area, including the Wherryman's Way, Angles Way and Weavers' Way.

A great route is the Wroxham to Coltishall walk, which follows the River Bure as it winds through peaceful meadows and woodlands. As you meander along the riverbank, you'll be treated to sweeping views of the water, dotted with boats sailing by, and the occasional kingfisher darting through.

Aside from these routes, there are also lots of stunning sites you can visit including Fairhaven Woodland and Water Garden, which boasts 4 miles of woodland pathways, a private broad and an abundance of wildlife such as water vole, hawks and butterflies. In fact, the area is said to be one of the best bird spotting locations in the country and is also home to many endangered and rare species such as cuckoo and bittern.

There are plenty of historic sites to visit too, including Burgh Castle, a third-century Roman fort with some of the best views in the area, and St Benet's Abbey near Ludham, the only monastery in England which was not closed down by Henry VIII. Best of all, both of these sites welcome dogs with open arms.

Places to explore

CRUISE ON THE BROADS
Broads Tours, The Bridge, NR12 8RX

Cruising down The Broads is hands down the best way to experience the beauty of this place, and there are plenty that are dog friendly. There are loads of places you can moor up for a picnic, lots of wildlife to spot, and photo opportunities in abundance as you sail across the water – look out for ruins, market towns and beautiful windmills. Broads Tours allow you to rent a boat if you're brave enough to take one out yourself, or if you'd prefer to just sit back and relax, you can hire a driver too.

FAIRHAVEN WOODLAND AND WATER GARDEN
School Road, South Walsham, NR13 6DZ

If wildlife is your thing, Fairhaven Woodland and Water Garden is the perfect day trip. It's open year-round and is home to beautiful plants and flowers including one of Norfolk's oldest trees, migrant birds and wildlife, many varieties of fungi and toadstools, kingfishers, deer and even otters. Once you set foot in the woodland you get a feeling of seclusion and peace, much like being in a secret garden.

WINTERTON BEACH
Beach Road, Winterton-on-Sea, NR29 4DD

With vast expanses of sand that back on to rolling dunes, Winterton Beach has a wonderful sense of openness to it. It's a huge area, which means it rarely feels crowded and most importantly dogs are welcome year-round.

Places to eat, drink and stay 🐾🐾

THE DOG INN
Johnson Street, Ludham, NR29 5NY

A wonderful dog and family friendly pub, The Dog Inn even offers a water station and waterproof dog beds for furry patrons. The pub is surrounded by walks, so makes for a fantastic stop off after exploring the local area.

THE SWAN INN
10 Lower Street, Horning, NR12 8AA

This beautifully timbered pub has bags of history and boasts an incredible view overlooking the River Bure. Enjoy cask ales and fine wines, alongside delicious dishes that change with the seasons, while you watch boaters and wildlife pass by.

THE LION INN AT THURNE
The Street, Thurne, NR29 3AP

With moorings right outside for your boat, The Lion Inn is a popular stop-off among locals and those on boating holidays. It's cosy and inviting inside, and the staff are always willing to recommend local walks right from the door.

SWAN COTTAGE
Whimpwell Street, Happisburgh, NR12 0QD

If you're looking for self-catering where dogs are welcomed with open arms, Swan Cottage is perfect. Dogs are allowed everywhere in the cottage with throws provided for the sofa. They even provide dog treats, towels, toys, poo bags, a doggy shower and more.

THE NORFOLK MEAD HOTEL
Church Loke, Coltishall, NR12 7DN

A boutique hotel and spa set in a beautiful Georgian House, The Norfolk Mead has several dog-friendly rooms and makes for the perfect luxury stay on The Broads. Plus, did I mention there is a welcome pack for humans and treats for dogs on arrival too?!

HERBERT WOODS
Bridge Road, Potter Heigham, NR29 5JF

Would I even be writing about the Norfolk Broads if I didn't have a boat holiday option on this list? Herbert Woods have a range of boats that you can hire, and the majority are dog friendly. You even receive a full safety briefing and tutorial on arrival as well as life jackets, so you'll feel confident cruising down the water.

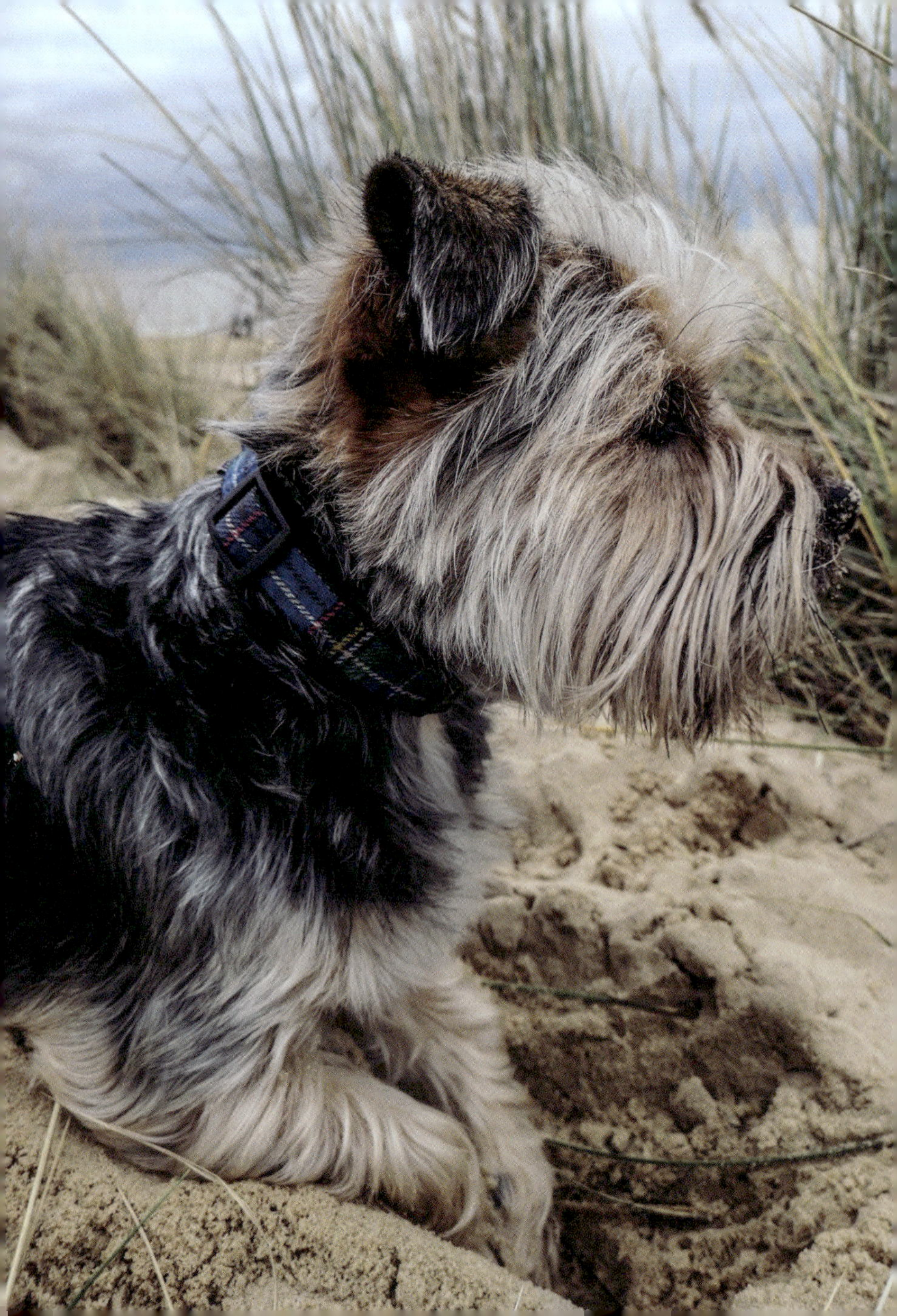

5.

Southwold

Southwold ticks all the quintessentially British seaside boxes. A sandy beach backed with colourful beach huts? Tick. A pier with traditional games? Tick. An abundance of great pubs and eateries? Tick.

In fact, it's one of my favourite places to visit on the Suffolk coast, mainly due to the number of fantastic walks you can take in the nearby area. The pace of life here is so relaxed, you will be able to ease into holiday mode in no time.

The prominent lighthouse in the town makes for a great photo backdrop. Standing 31 metres tall and Grade II listed, it's still working; guiding boats as they navigate the east coast.

It's also home to Adnams Brewery, so you know you'll never be far away from a good beer. The brewing rooms are set next to the lighthouse, where there is a dog-friendly flagship store and café. If you like your beer, the shop is well worth a visit, with a range of beers and ales, locally sourced gins and vodkas, and quirky gifts.

The pier is another must while visiting. It's iconic and eccentric in equal measure, with a fantastic arcade filled to the brim with traditional seaside games like the twopenny shove machine, air hockey, hall of mirrors and more. Plus, the views of the surrounding coast and town from here are pretty special. You can enjoy the atmosphere while tucking into a portion of fresh fish and chips – it doesn't get much better!

Southwold is fantastically located, meaning you're in perfect position to explore some of the other amazing towns and villages along this beautiful stretch of coastline, including the wonderful Aldeburgh and Dunwich Heath.

One of my favourite walks here is around the National Trust owned Dunwich Heath and Beach, which in the summer months is alive with pink and purple heather and coconut-scented yellow gorse. Afterwards, The Ship Inn is a must-visit – the perfect coastal pub with great locally sourced food, and you can even stay here too, as all their rooms are dog friendly.

The nearby idyllic seaside town of Walberswick is also within walking distance of Southwold itself, and is well worth a visit. It's a beautiful Georgian village, which is a lot quieter than Southwold, with a long shingle beach and nature reserve, and you can even get a ferry over to save you the walk.

Places to explore

SOUTHWOLD PIER
North Parade, IP18 6BN

A quintessentially British seaside attraction, the pier at Southwold is lined with quirky shops, traditional amusements, and cafés, all with a nostalgic touch that harks back to the golden age of seaside holidays. Dogs are welcome to stroll along the pier and take in the fresh sea air and stunning coastal views too.

WALBERSWICK FERRY
42 Ferry Road, IP18 6NB

Take the hand-rowed ferry across the River Blyth to the charming village of Walberswick where you'll find miles of scenic walking routes to explore filled with windswept dunes, salt marshes and heathlands that define this Area of Outstanding Natural Beauty.

DUNWICH HEATH
Coastguard Cottages, Minsmere Road, IP17 3DJ

This National Trust site is a patchwork of heather-clad heathland, coastal cliffs and woodland trails, making the perfect backdrop for long scenic walks. As you wander the winding paths you'll be greeted by vibrant wildflowers and, if you're lucky, the call of rare birds, like the Dartford warbler.

Places to eat, drink and stay 🐾🐾

ADNAMS CAFÉ
4 Drayman Square, Victoria Street, IP18 6GB

The perfect spot for lunch, Adnams Café is nestled in the heart of Southwold on the site of the Adnams Brewery. While your dog enjoys the cosy atmosphere, you can indulge in their hot chocolate, which is rich, creamy and topped with lashings of whipped cream!

THE LORD NELSON
42 East Street, IP18 6EJ

The Lord Nelson (or 'The Nellie' as this pub is more affectionately known), is a social hub in the centre of Southwold right on the seafront. If you like beer, this is a fantastic place to visit, boasting an extensive award-winning Adnams menu. They also have a great pizza menu, and dogs are welcomed throughout.

THE FARMSTEAD LODGES
Kettleburgh Road, Easton, IP13 0EL

Luxury dog-friendly lodges surrounded by the rolling Suffolk countryside, The Farmstead Lodges are a great option for a romantic getaway. There is a dog walking space on site, and for the humans, a decadent outdoor bath.

THE WESTLETON CROWN
The Street, Westleton, IP17 3AD

Sitting on the edge of an immaculate village green, The Westleton Crown dates as far back as the twelfth century. All their rooms are designed specifically with dogs in mind, with bedding and treats provided. It's also a great place for a bite to eat, serving hearty meals by an open roaring fire, and they even have a dog menu with cooked sausages.

THE SHIP INN AT DUNWICH
St James's Street, Dunwich, IP17 3DT

When you imagine the perfect coastal pub and inn, The Ship Inn at Dunwich definitely comes to mind. Located in the sleepy village of Dunwich you're also only a short stroll from the beautiful beach where dogs are permitted year-round. It's dog friendly throughout and boasts a range of beautiful rooms.

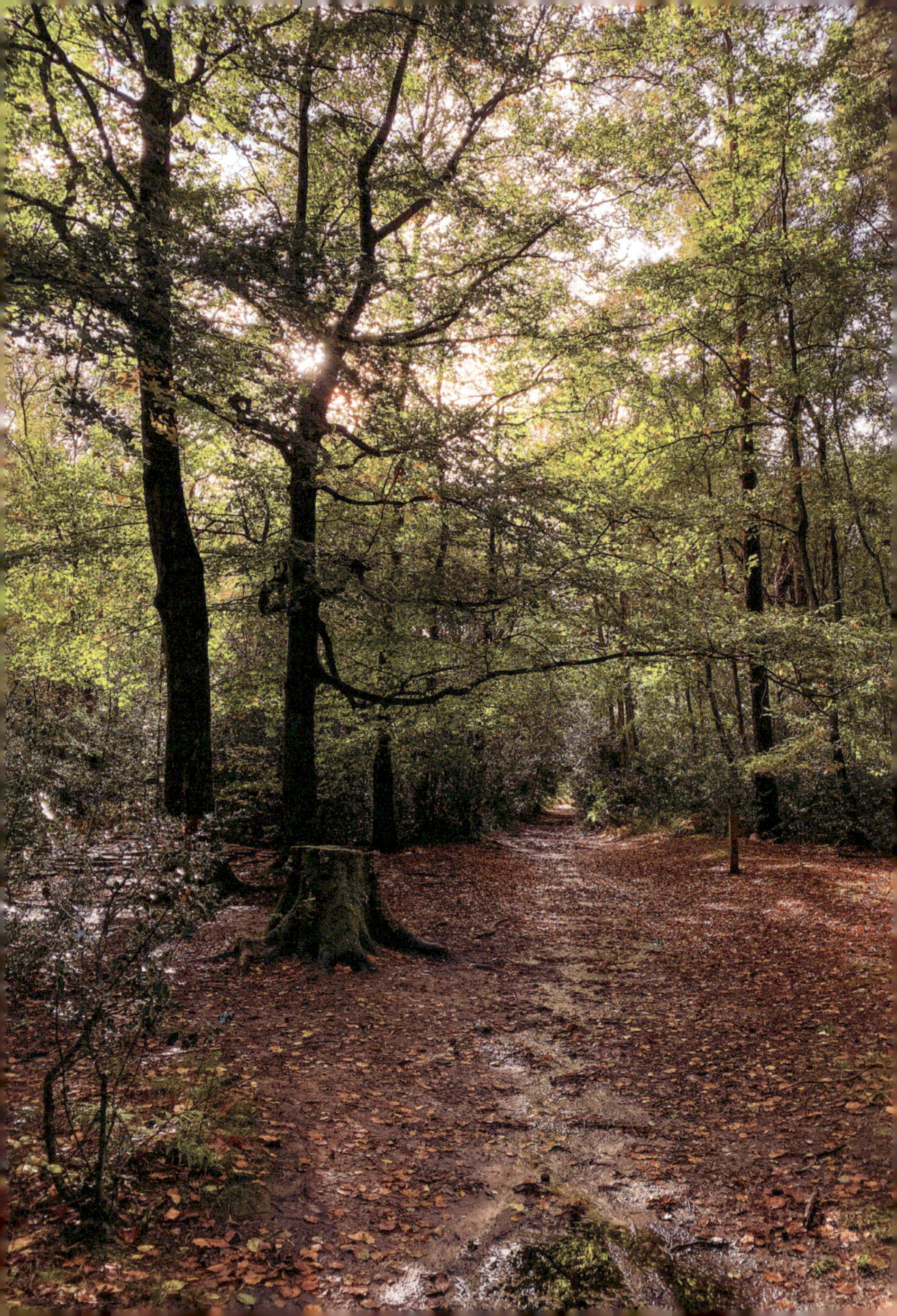

6.

Holt

One of the most attractive towns in Norfolk, Holt is home to charming eighteenth-century Georgian buildings housing art galleries, book shops and amazing places to eat along a long high street with hidden magical courtyards.

The high street itself is full of history, with loads of independent shops to explore where dogs are not only allowed, but often greeted with treats and affection. It's also home to Bakers & Larners, an iconic department store that has been around for over 250 years.

A must-visit is Holt Country Park, a 100-acre woodland with a range of walking routes and trails to follow, and just a short walk away from the town. If you're lucky you might even spot one of the elusive wild ponies that roam the beautiful open heathland. The diverse wildlife, such as woodpeckers and muntjac deer, alongside the changing seasonal scenery make every visit to the park a new adventure.

Nearby Spout Hills also makes for a magical place to visit just a short walk out of town. This picturesque nature reserve features rolling hills and lush meadows, with plenty of space for dogs to explore and run off-lead. The former reservoir site has been transformed into a natural haven, with numerous springs and bubbling brooks flowing through the area, making it the perfect place for a walk with your dog.

There are a range of events that take place here throughout the year, including Holt Festival in the summer, a fantastic Christmas light event, and Sunday markets that showcase the best of local independent makers.

Although there is an abundance to see and do right in the town, Holt is perfectly placed with fantastic connections across the area.

If you're looking for a day trip with a difference, I highly recommend checking out North Norfolk Railway who offer dog-friendly train trips on their heritage steam and diesel railway between Holt and Sheringham. The scenic journey takes you through the heart of Norfolk's countryside, with views of lush farmland, wild beauty and occasional glimpses of the shimmering sea in the distance.

Nearby, Felbrigg Hall is also well worth a visit with extensive parkland and woodland to explore. Dogs are welcome on leads throughout the majority of the estate, including the scenic trails that wind through the 520 acres, passing peaceful lakes and ancient trees with a range of clearly waymarked routes.

Places to explore

HOLT COUNTRY PARK

Edgefield Hill, NR25 6SP

A serene country park just a mile or so out of town, Holt Country Park is the perfect setting for walks with a range of trails you can take. The park spans 100 acres of diverse landscapes, including forests and open heathlands, and is dotted with charming sculptures to spot on your way. There is also a great on-site café where dogs are welcome and where you can pick up a tasty slice of homemade cake.

NORTH NORFOLK RAILWAY

Cromer Road, NR25 6QR

This heritage steam railway runs between the delightful towns of Holt and Sheringham, providing breathtaking views of the surrounding landscapes. Dogs are welcomed on board, and it makes for the perfect adventure for you and your canine companion. There are scenic stops along the route with loads of dog-friendly walks to explore.

FELBRIGG HALL

Norwich, NR11 8PR

A stunning National Trust property and one of the most beautiful estates in the region, Felbrigg boasts over 520 acres to explore – including ancient woodlands, rolling parkland and a tranquil lake. You'll find an abundance of walking trails to take, from gentle strolls to more challenging hikes. The Victory V Walk, in particular, offers a scenic route through the heart of the estate, with inspiring views and plenty of wildlife to spot along the way.

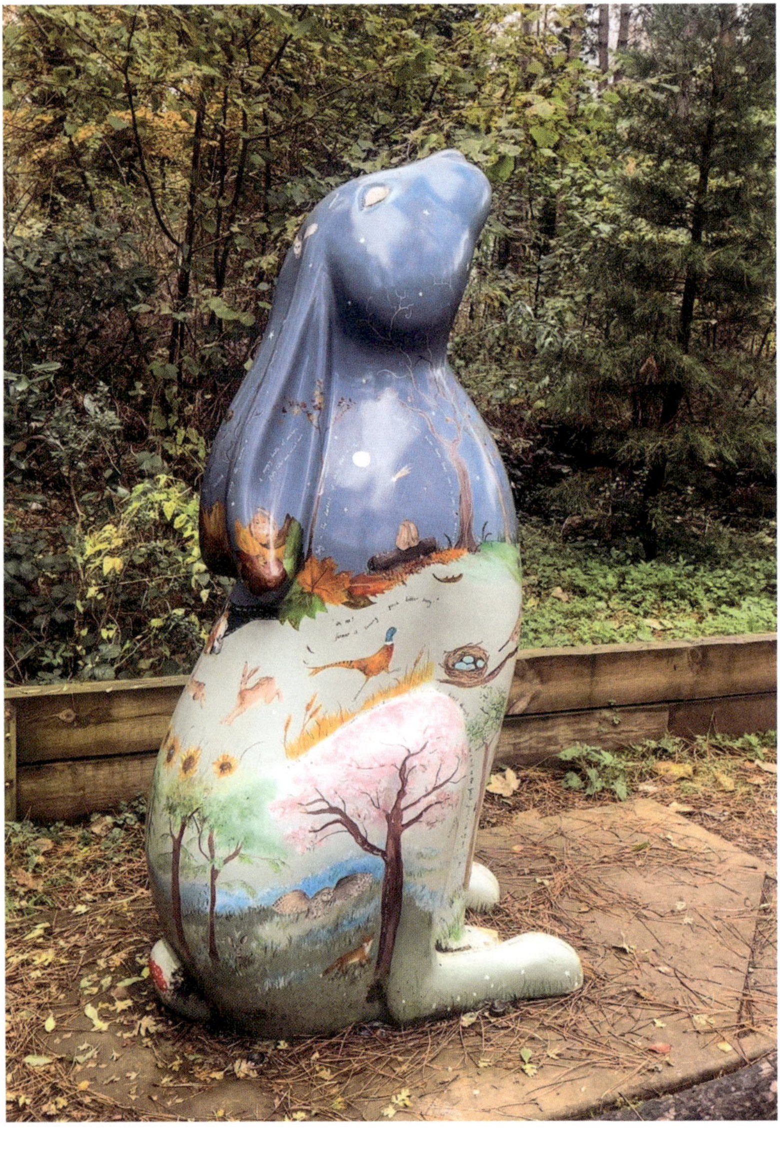

Places to eat, drink and stay 🐾🐾

TWO MAGPIES BAKERY
27 High Street, NR25 6BN

When you see the gorgeous baked goods piled high in the window you won't be able to walk past Two Magpies Bakery without going inside. They serve a range of delicious pastries and sweet treats, with brunch and lunch menus too, inside a modern and chic café, which is dog friendly throughout.

THE KING'S HEAD
19 High Street, NR25 6BN

A traditional Gastropub with dog treats on the bar, The King's Head is perfectly located on the high street, making it a great stop-off in between exploring. It serves proper hearty food and, if the weather is on your side, has a lovely outdoor terrace where you can watch the world go by.

HETTY'S HOUSE TEA ROOM
Holt Country Park, Norwich Road, NR25 6SP

Nestled in Holt Country Park, Hetty's House Tea Room offers a range of freshly prepared treats from scrumptious homemade cakes and scones to hearty sandwiches and light lunches. It is surrounded by the trails of the park, making it a great spot to stop off after a stomp around the woods.

THE FEATHERS
6 Market Place, NR25 6BW

Combining historic charm with modern comfort, The Feathers' friendly staff go out of their way to make sure you and your dog feel at home, with water bowls and treats on arrival. There are a range of dedicated dog-friendly rooms, which come with everything you need, including cosy dog beds and easy access to outdoor areas.

CLEY WINDMILL
The Quay, Cley-next-the-Sea, NR25 7RP

A historic eighteenth-century windmill that has been lovingly restored into an inviting bed and breakfast, Cley Windmill offers a place to stay with a difference. It has distinctive architecture, rustic charm, and stunning coastal views, plus a perfectly welcoming atmosphere with dogs allowed in most areas. Located right on the North Norfolk Coastal Path it makes for an ideal base for exploring the nearby marshes, villages and beaches.

KELLING HEATH HOLIDAY PARK
NR25 7HW

Surrounded by natural beauty, Kelling Health Holiday Park offers a range of accommodation options including luxury lodges and spacious caravans, to woodland pitches for camping and touring. Just a short distance from Holt, the park is a tranquil escape with plenty of woodland trails and heathland to explore.

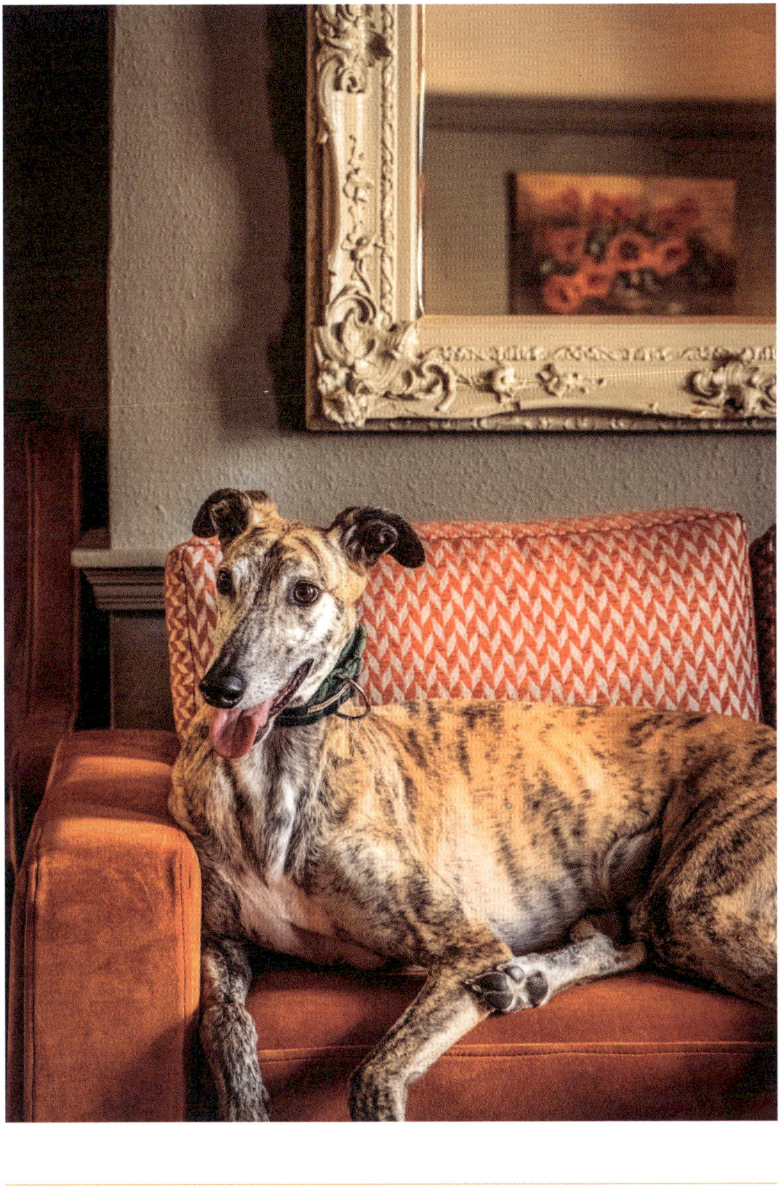

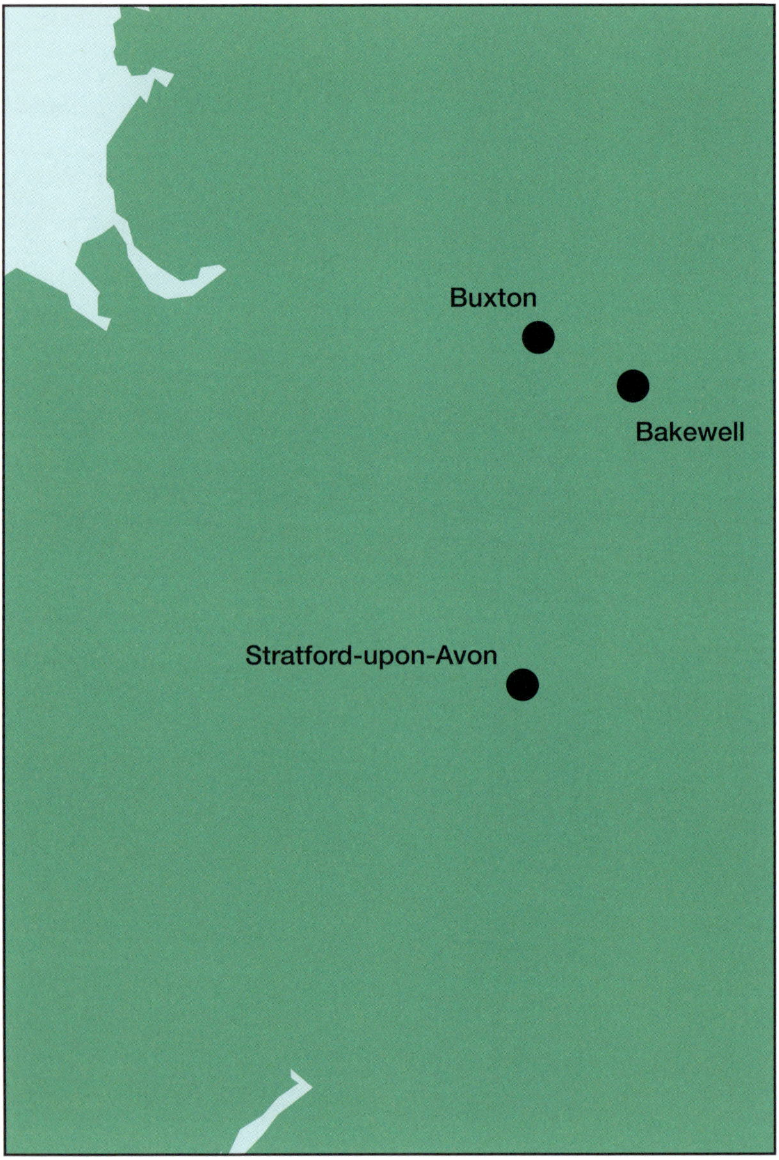
Buxton
Bakewell
Stratford-upon-Avon

Midlands

Bakewell   53
Stratford-upon-Avon   61
Buxton   67

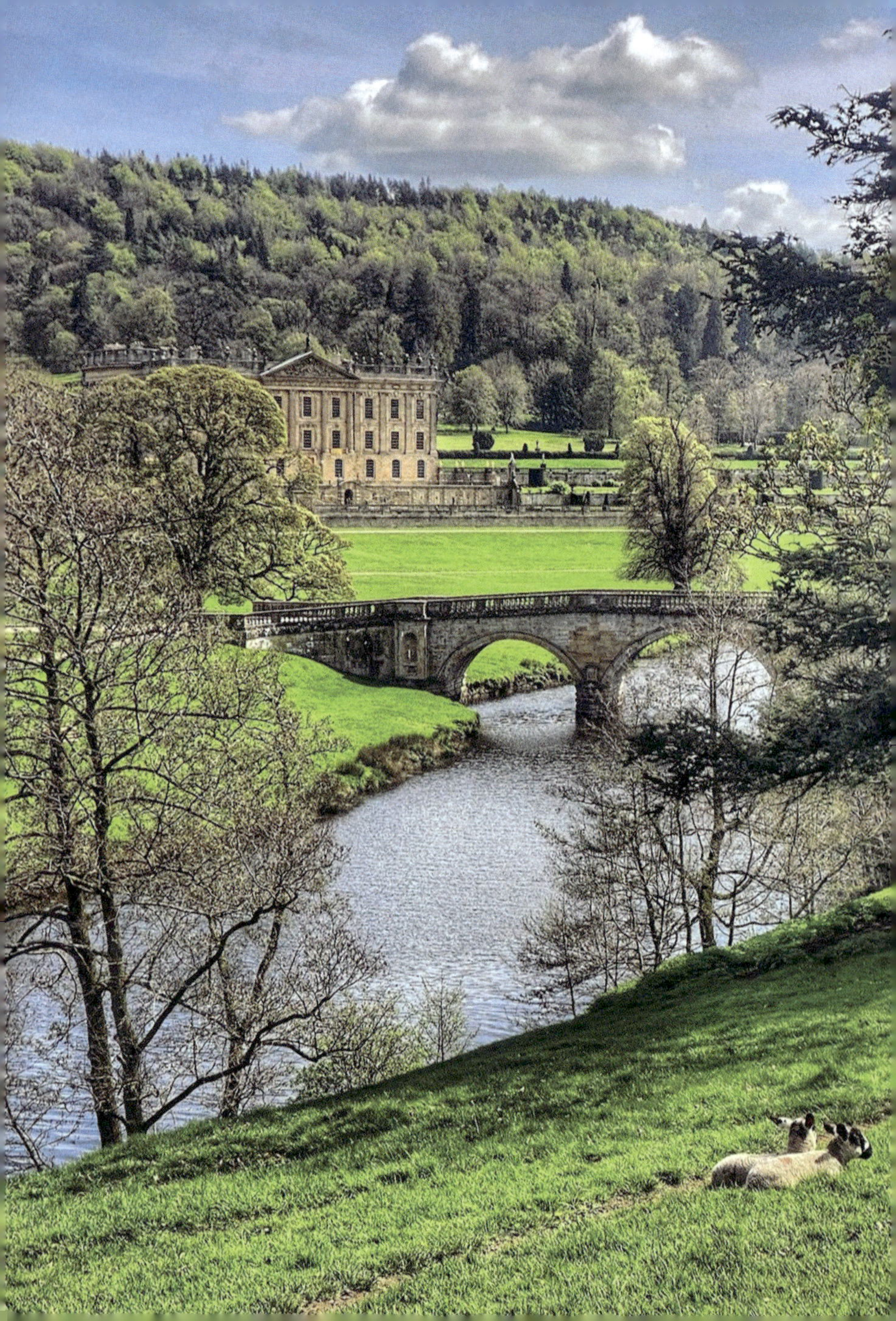

7.

Bakewell

Conveniently located on the edge of the Peak District National Park, Bakewell is a charming market town surrounded by beautiful walking routes and picturesque landscapes.

Just a short walk from the town centre you're able to join the Monsal Trail, an 8.5-mile route that runs through the stunning surrounding countryside and through deserted tunnels. Running down a disused railway track, the trail is easy to walk and suitable for pushchairs.

There are plenty of great stop-offs on the route, including the Hassop Station Café and Thornbridge Outdoors, which has a great café, a small free petting farm and beautiful gardens, which are also dog friendly to visit.

Bakewell is also close to Chatsworth House, one of the best-kept stately homes in the country and one you'll probably recognise from the likes of Pride and Prejudice and The Duchess. It's a must-visit for dog owners exploring the South Peak District, with a huge rolling estate to explore and fantastic walks.

While dogs are not permitted inside the main house, they are allowed in the expansive gardens and parkland surrounding the estate, with miles of walking trails. They even have a great dog-friendly Christmas light display in the winter too, which is well worth a visit.

In the town itself you'll find an abundance of fantastic shops and great dog-friendly pubs and cafés. Although not dog friendly inside, no trip to Bakewell is quite complete without grabbing an authentic Bakewell pudding from the historic Old Original Bakewell Pudding Shop.

The origins of the iconic treat date back to the early nineteenth century, where legend has it that a cook mistakenly mixed up a sponge cake recipe with a jam tart, resulting in the now famous pudding that has become a local delicacy.

Nearby you'll also find some other lovely towns and villages to visit including Matlock Bath, a popular destination for families and starting point for some fantastic walks such as the tranquil Riverside Walk along the River Derwent where dogs can enjoy a splash in the water.

For the more adventurous, there are also more strenuous routes such as the High Tor Walk, providing spectacular views across Matlock and beyond, and the Lovers' Walk, a scenic route that takes you through a wooded valley and along the banks of the river. Plus, a visit to the Heights of Abraham in a dog-friendly cable car is a must.

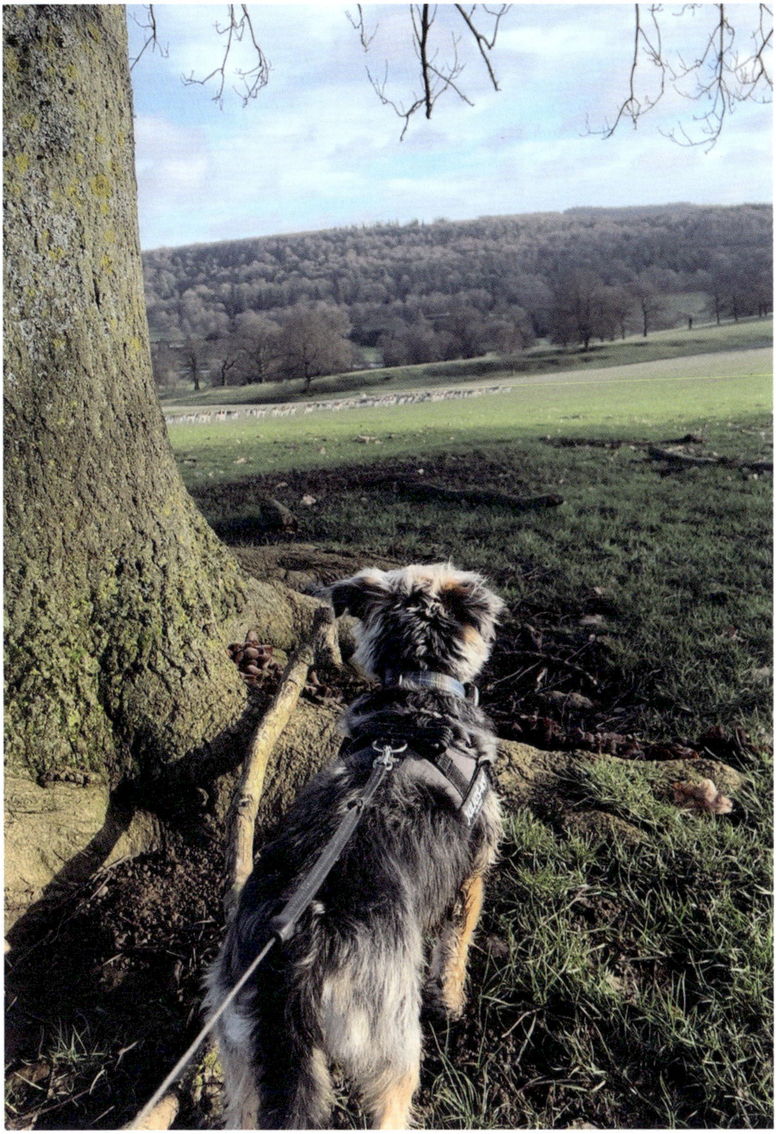

Places to explore

MONSAL TRAIL
Bakewell Station, 6 Station Road, DE45 1GE

Following the route of a former railway line, the Monsal Trail provides a relatively flat walk through the spectacular Peak District landscape. As you meander the trail you'll be treated to breathtaking views of lush valleys, dramatic limestone gorges and picturesque viaducts.

CHATSWORTH HOUSE
Chatsworth, DE45 1PP

A magnificent stately home nestled in the heart of Derbyshire's Peak District, Chatsworth has over 1,000 acres of beautifully landscaped grounds to explore. Dogs are allowed in the expansive gardens, which include sculptures, fountains, manicured lawns and the famous Cascade water feature, as well as the wider estate where you can enjoy longer walks through rolling pastures and ancient woodlands.

HEIGHTS OF ABRAHAM
Dale Road, Matlock, DE4 3NT

Have you ever been on a cable car with your dog? This is a unique attraction that offers stunning views, and when you reach the top, you'll find woodland walks with well-maintained paths and gardens, alongside a wonderful dog-friendly café.

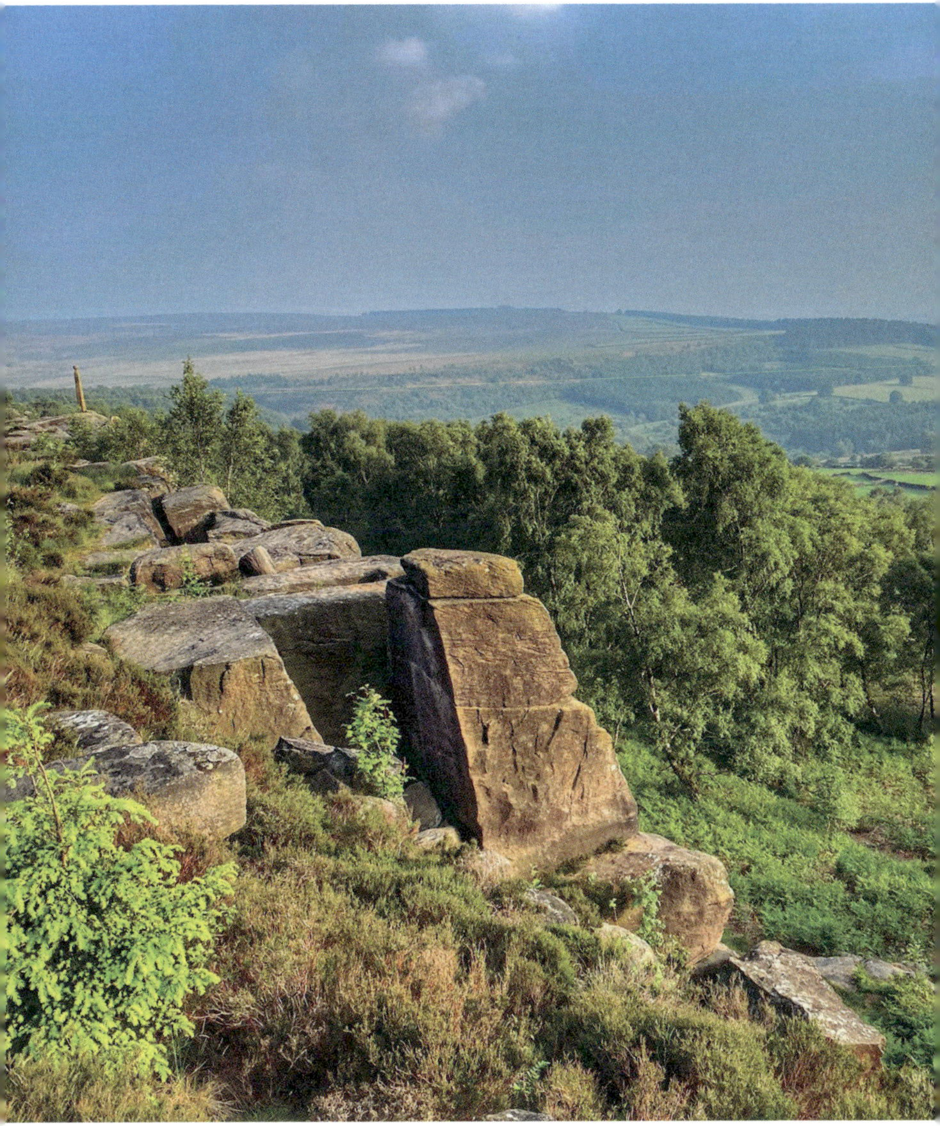

Places to eat, drink and stay 🐾🐾

THORNBRIDGE BREWERY TAP ROOM
Riverside Brewery, Buxton Road, DE45 1GS

Well-loved sofas and chairs fill this vast brewery, which boasts a relaxed and friendly atmosphere. You'll be able to enjoy a pint of award-winning craft beer and a freshly cooked pizza from their wood-fired oven, while you'll find treats and water bowls for your dog to enjoy.

THE WHITE LION
Main Street, Great Longstone, DE45 1TA

The White Lion oozes traditional country pub charm and warmly welcomes dogs and humans alike. It's an ideal stop on a long walk, with a roaring open fire to welcome you on winter days. There is a great menu of classic British fare made from locally sourced ingredients.

EDENSOR TEA COTTAGE
Edensor, DE45 1PH

Set in the charming village of Edensor on the Chatsworth Estate, Edensor Tea Cottage is the perfect place to enjoy a traditional afternoon tea or light lunch. Dogs are welcome inside and out, although make sure to book ahead or avoid peak times.

PEAK EDGE HOTEL
Darley Road, S45 0LW

A luxurious boutique hotel combining modern comfort with rustic charm, The Peak Edge Hotel is fantastically located to enjoy the Peaks. There are dedicated dog-friendly rooms, and beautiful grounds to explore. Onsite you'll also find the dog-friendly AA Rosette Awarded restaurant, The Red Lion, which is an ideal spot to enjoy a luxury meal.

BAKEWELL RETREATS
Monyash Road, DE45 1JE

Bakewell Retreats offer a collection of wonderful dog-friendly accommodation in both the centre of Bakewell and further afield. Their cottages in Bakewell town centre provide a fantastic location, while their complex of cottages on Monyash Road offer spacious accommodations surrounded by beautiful countryside, complete with access to an on-site heated swimming pool.

STONELOW COTTAGE
Chesterfield Road, Baslow, DE45 1PQ

A beautifully refurbished farmhouse, Stonelow is an idyllic retreat a short drive from Bakewell itself. Surrounded by the rolling hills of the Derbyshire Dales you'll find sweeping countryside views of Eastmoor from every window. Plus, entry tickets to Chatsworth are included with stays here.

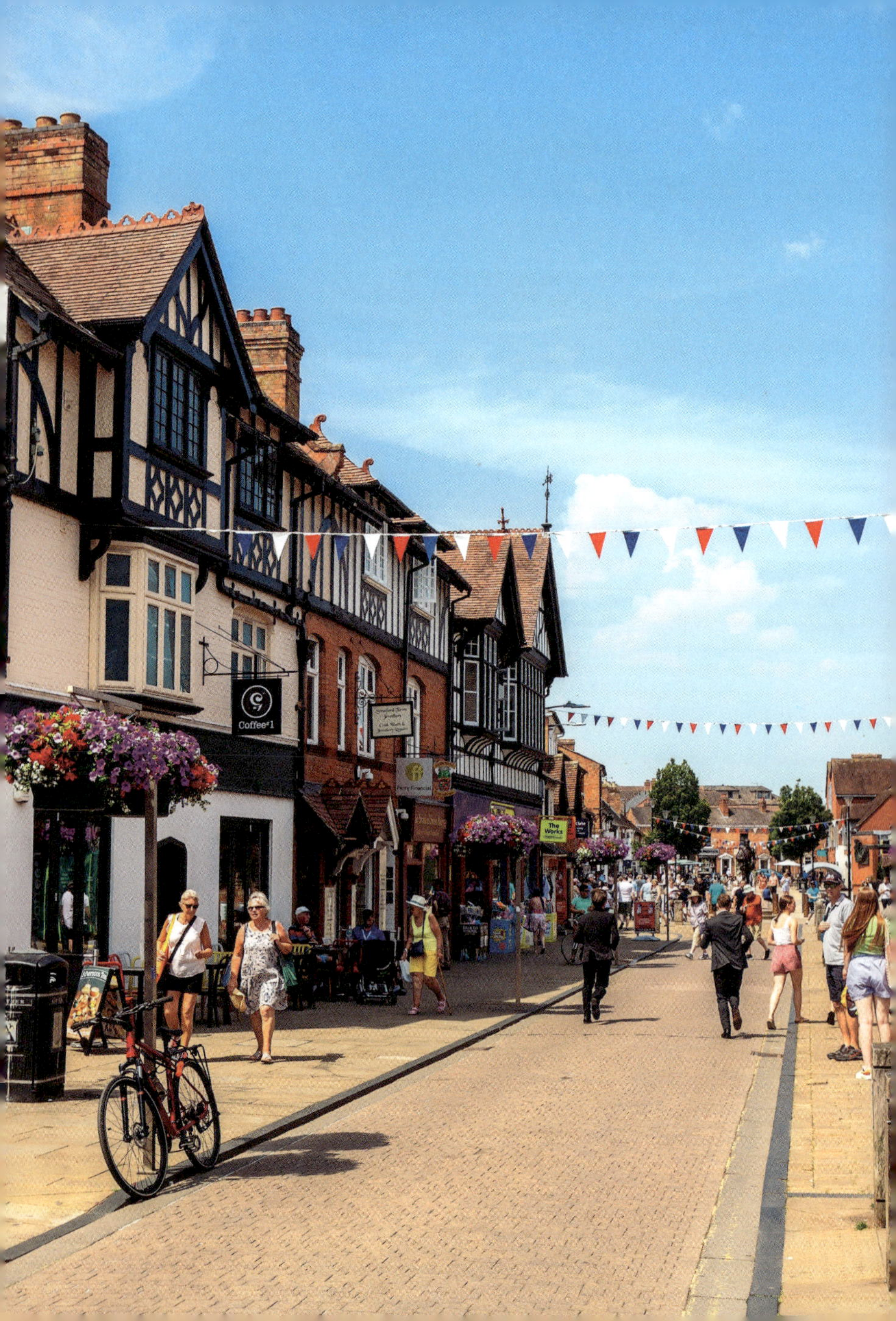
Coffee#1
The Works

8.

Stratford-upon-Avon

Birthplace of William Shakespeare, you could be forgiven for thinking you'd stepped into a time machine when visiting this quaint market town. Stratford-upon-Avon is home to many 800-year-old buildings, giving you a real sense of what the town would have looked like when Shakespeare himself roamed the streets.

A haven for literary enthusiasts, the town is also a delightful destination for dog lovers, with a range of dog-friendly activities, restaurants and bars.

One of the most enjoyable ways to experience Stratford-upon-Avon is by walking along the banks of the River Avon. Lined with scenic paths, you'll be able to watch as narrowboats glide by and enjoy the peaceful sounds of nature.

The Bancroft Gardens Theatre also offer a lovely green space where dogs are welcome to roam. The gardens provide opportunity to stretch your legs while enjoying views of the river and the iconic Royal Shakespeare Theatre. During the summer months, the garden is often host to open-air events and performances, adding a cultural touch to your visit.

The town's many historic sites are also accommodating to dogs. The Shakespeare Birthplace Trust welcomes dogs in their gardens and lots of their outdoor areas. Additionally, the nearby Anne Hathaway's Cottage is a stunning setting with extensive gardens to walk. You can also pick up the Shakespeare's Stratford Walk, a self-guided tour, which takes you past significant landmarks related to Shakespeare's life and works.

If you're visiting in the summer, keep an eye out for local events and festivals, such as the Stratford River Festival, which features live music, food stalls and family friendly activities where dogs are more than welcome.

There are also a range of walks you can take right from the town centre. A particular favourite of mine being the Stratford Greenway Walk, a 5-mile circular route which takes you through meadows, woodlands and along the banks of the river, passing the famous Holy Trinity Church where Shakespeare is buried.

Places to explore

CHARLECOTE PARK

Wellesbourne, CV35 9ER

A stunning National Trust property located just a few miles from Stratford-upon-Avon, Charlecote Park offers a variety of walks through its extensive deer park and along the River Avon. If you're lucky, you'll get the chance to spot the historic herd of fallow deer that have roamed the grounds for centuries grazing peacefully across the beautiful rolling landscape.

STRATFORD GREENWAY

Old Town, CV37 9AL

Starting right from the centre of town, Stratford Greenway is a 5-mile traffic-free trail following a former railway line, making it perfect if you're travelling with a pushchair. There are plenty of opportunities for doggy sniffs as the beautiful route passes through lush meadows and the serene Warwickshire countryside. Along the trail, keep a look out for a variety of wildlife including rabbits darting through the fields, and birds such as skylarks, finches and the occasional heron.

SHAKESPEARE'S BIRTHPLACE

Henley Street, CV37 6QW

Dedicated to preserving the legacy of the famous playwright William Shakespeare, Shakespeare's Birthplace is a must-visit for anyone eager to explore the town's rich history. While dogs are not permitted inside the historic houses, they are warmly welcomed in the picturesque gardens of Shakespeare's Birthplace, Hall's Croft and Anne Hathaway's Cottage. Both are beautifully maintained outdoor spaces that provide a lovely setting for a stroll, and plenty of shade if the weather is warm.

Places to eat, drink and stay 🐾🐾

THE ARDEN HOTEL
Chapel Lane, Waterside, CV37 6BA

If you're looking for luxury, you might just have found it. This boutique hotel combines timeless elegance with modern comforts, and even includes dogs in the five-star treatment too. You can expect a doggy bag with treats and a toy, dog bed, dog bowls and even a sausage at breakfast.

BOBBY'S CAFÉ
The Stratford Greenway, Seven Meadows Road, CV37 9LE

Housed in a quirky converted railway carriage, Bobby's is located along the scenic Stratford Greenway, making a fantastic pit stop during a walk. The café welcomes dogs with open arms, providing water bowls, dog treats and lots of fuss!

SWAN'S NEST HOTEL
Banbury Road, Bridge Foot, CV37 7LT

Located along the banks of the River Avon, Swan's Nest Hotel is in a fantastic location for exploring the town and its iconic attractions. It has an enclosed garden plus a welcome treat of a ball and a bone – they know the way to a dog's heart!

DIRTY DUCK
Waterside, CV37 6BA

Formally The Black Swan, this eighteenth-century pub has long been a favourite of actors and theatregoers, with walls covered in photos of famous thespians. Dogs are warmly welcomed in the bar area, although if the weather is nice, head to the riverside garden.

ROWLEY FARM HOLIDAYS
Ockeridge Lane, Worcester, WR6 6LY

Located a little way out of Stratford-upon-Avon, Rowley Farm is worth the drive. You'll find beautifully restored accommodation with hot tubs, and everything you could need to make sure your dog is at home including bowls, treats and even blankets to put on the furniture.

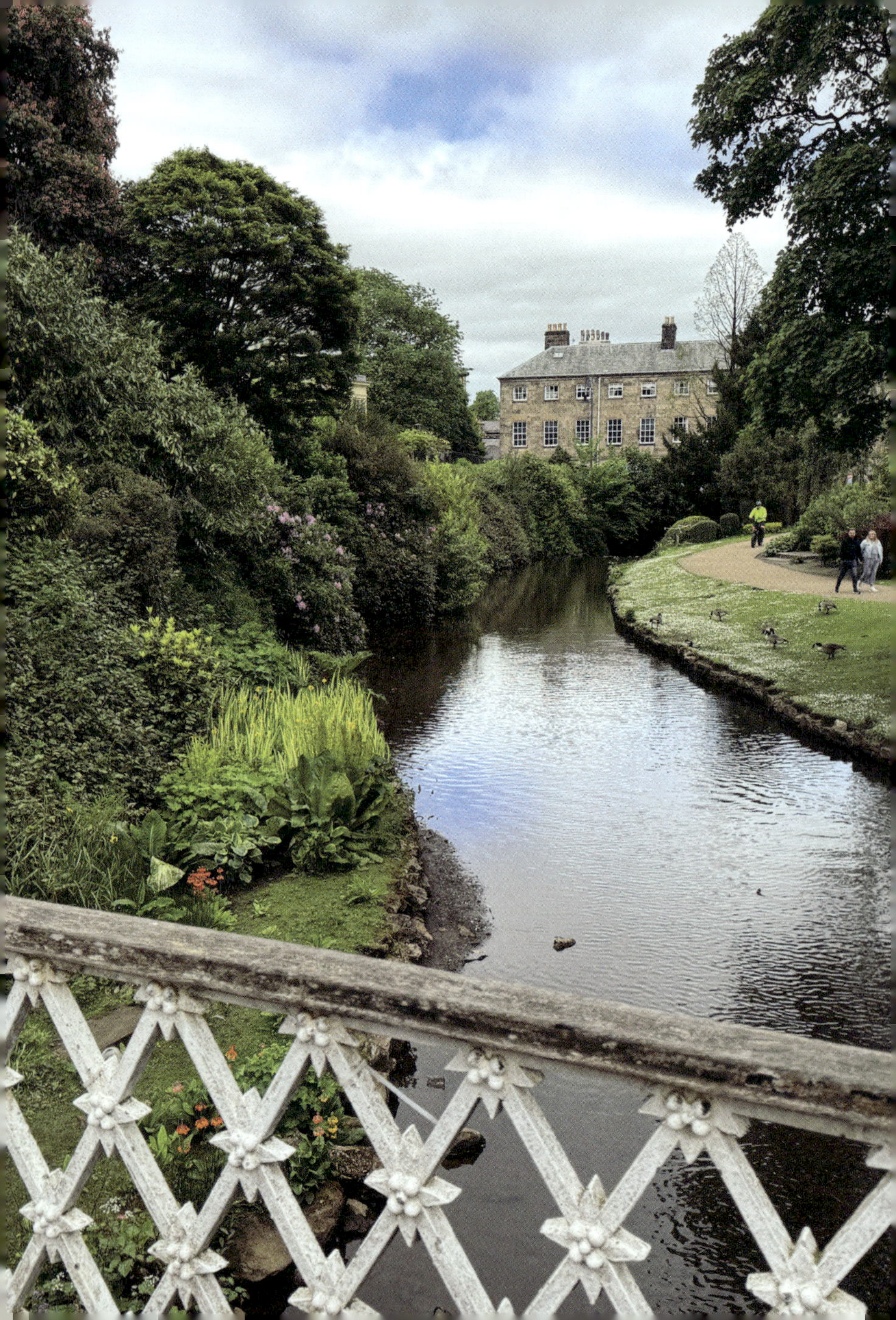

9.

Buxton

In the heart of the Peak District you'll find Buxton, a charming and bustling town known for its Georgian architecture and natural springs. It's an ideal place for a dog-friendly break as there is a plethora of activities and attractions nearby, alongside easy access to some of the best walks in the country.

The town's centrepiece is the Buxton Crescent, which you can admire as you wander towards the nearby Pavilion Gardens. A perfect Grade-II listed Victorian park, you'll find 23 acres of expansive lawns and gardens to explore alongside a lake where you can even hire a pedalo.

Throughout the town you'll also find a range of dog-friendly shops and eateries, with many of the pubs more than happy to accommodate canine patrons.

If you're somewhat of a coffee connoisseur, The Dandelion Café should definitely be on your hit list. They serve a plethora of speciality brews, have a cake cabinet filled to the brim with mouthwatering treats and will treat your dog as if they are guests in their own right!

The surrounding natural landscape is a dog walker's paradise, offering a variety of trails suitable for all skill levels. Nestled in the High Peak area, it's renowned for its dramatic scenery, including vast moorlands and rugged hills, and is one of those places where everywhere you turn, there is a stunning photo opportunity.

One of the highlights is the High Peak Trail, another former railway line that stretches out for 17 miles all the way to Cromford, offering a relatively flat route that allows for a leisurely walk, while still taking in the spectacular views of the surrounding countryside.

For those looking for something a bit more challenging, Kinder Scout, the highest point in the Peak District, is also nearby. While the walk can be quite demanding with some rocky paths and steep gradients, the panoramic views from the summit are well worth it with heather-clad moorlands and the picturesque Kinder Downfall waterfall adding to the appeal.

Just a short drive away The Derwent Valley has an array of walks with rich history and serene reservoirs. One of the highlights is Ladybower Reservoir, a popular destination where dogs and their owners can enjoy an array of scenic trails along the water's edge, weaving through woodlands and pine trees.

If you fancy something a bit different, Poole's Cavern, a natural limestone cave, is completely dog friendly to visit. As you meander through the cavern's chamber of intricate passageways, you'll be able to see impressive stalactites and stalagmites that sparkle with a magical glow, alongside fascinating rock formations.

From here you can also walk to Solomon's Temple, a historic hilltop tower and rewarding walk with views of the surrounding countryside. The short but steep climb takes you through enchanting woodland before opening up to a grassy landscape leading to the iconic Victorian structure. Once at the top you'll be able to enjoy sweeping vistas across the Peak District, with Buxton nestled below.

You'll also find some fantastic towns and villages within a short drive, such as Castleton, known for being the starting point to hikes such as Mam Tor and the Great Ridge, and Leek, where you can pick up the route to the well-known Roaches. A photographer's paradise, the rich heather and bilberry-dominated landscape bursts into colour in spring, creating a beautiful contrast against the grey granite rocks.

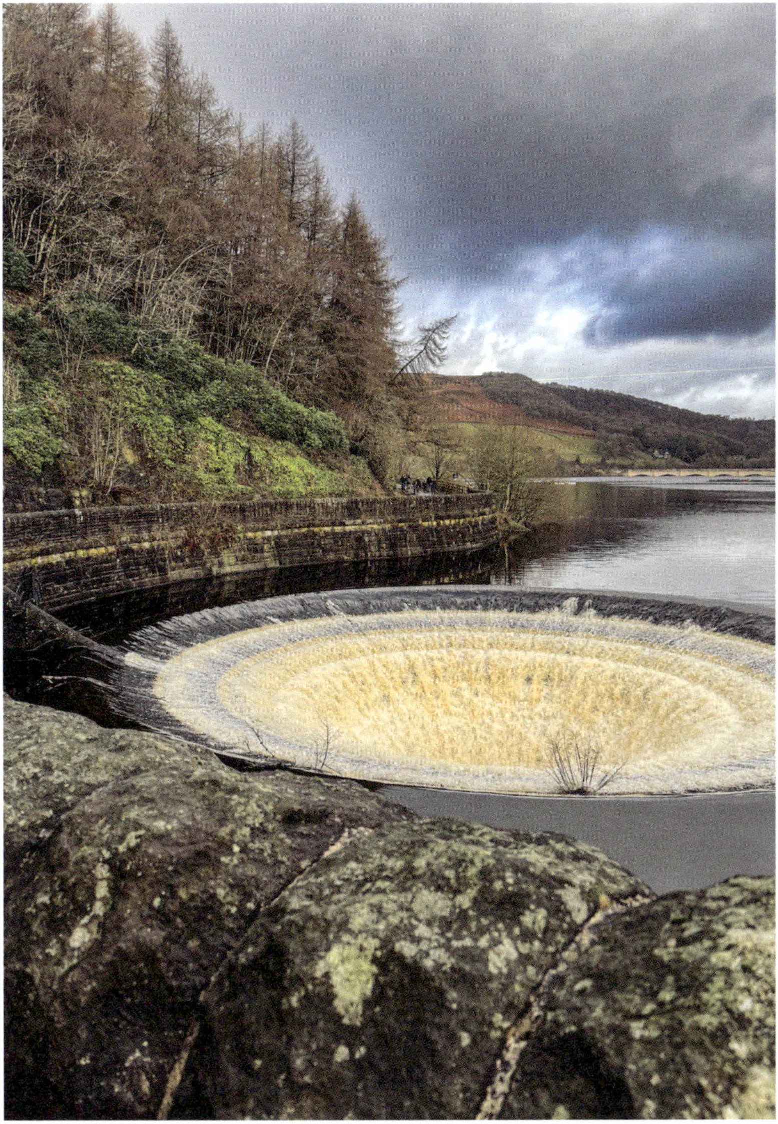

Places to explore

THE PAVILION GARDENS

St John's Road, SK17 6BE

Manicured gardens, winding paths and a serene ornamental lake, this 23-acre Victorian-era park is a fantastic spot to enjoy a stroll. As you wander through, you'll encounter bridges, a bandstand and the iconic glasshouse, home to exotic plants.

POOLE'S CAVERN

Green Lane, SK17 9DH

A fascinating underground wonder, Poole's Cavern offers a glimpse into the mysterious world beneath the Peak District. The limestone cave, rich with stunning stalactites and stalagmites is dog friendly all day with guided tours that take you deep into the cavern's chambers.

MAM TOR

Mam Nick Car Park, Castleton, Hope Valley, S33 8WA

Known affectionately as the 'Shivering Mountain' this breathtaking route is a must-do in the area. Despite towering at 516 metres, Mam Tor is a relatively easy climb with steps up, making it a perfect walk for dogs and humans of all abilities. At the summit you'll be rewarded with panoramic views of the Hope Valley and if you're lucky you might even spot birds like skylarks or kestrels soaring overhead.

Places to eat, drink and stay 🐾🐾

DANDELION CAFÉ
5 Grove Parade, SK17 6AJ

A haven for coffee lovers and just around the corner from The Pavilion Gardens, this dog-friendly café offers a warm atmosphere with rustic charm and friendly staff who will definitely make a fuss of your pooch. You'll find a huge coffee menu here and a specials board alongside a freshly baked desserts cabinet.

THE BULL'S HEAD
Church Street, Monyash, DE45 1JH

A proper village pub, The Bull's Head is a short drive from Buxton and is a fantastic place to unwind after exploring the nearby Lathkill Dale. It exudes a laid-back vibe and ticks all the quintessential boxes with exposed wooden beams, stone floor, roaring fireplace and a fantastic beer garden.

BANK COTTAGE
Eagle Street, SK17 6ER

Pretty and traditional, Bank Cottage is perfectly hidden in the middle of the bustling Buxton town. It has a great enclosed garden and the views of the town's beautiful golden hue limestone buildings transport you back to a bygone era.

THE OLD HALL HOTEL
The Square, SK17 6BD

Reputed to be the oldest hotel in England, you won't be surprised to read this is a hotel steeped in history. Located next to the beautiful Pavilion Gardens it's the perfect base for exploring the area's scenic walks. Dogs are welcomed here, with staff giving them plenty of fuss and attention.

THE BUXTON BREWERY TAP HOUSE
Old Court House, George Street, SK17 6AY

Perfect for those who appreciate craft beer, the Tap House is the home of Buxton Brewery, offering a rotating selection of their finest brews on tap. The food menu is equally as impressive with locally sourced pub-style fare. Dogs are welcomed in the bar area, making it a fantastic spot to enjoy a pint and a bite to eat.

RIVENDALE LODGE RETREAT
Buxton Road, Alsop en la Dale, Ashbourne, DE6 1QU

Rivendale is tucked away in the heart of the Peak District and is perfect for exploring the local walking routes in the area including the Tissington Trail. They have a range of different lodges but my favourite has to be the treehouse option, which is dreamily secluded and complete with a hot tub.

Keswick

Grasmere

Manchester

North West

Keswick	77
Grasmere	85
Manchester	91

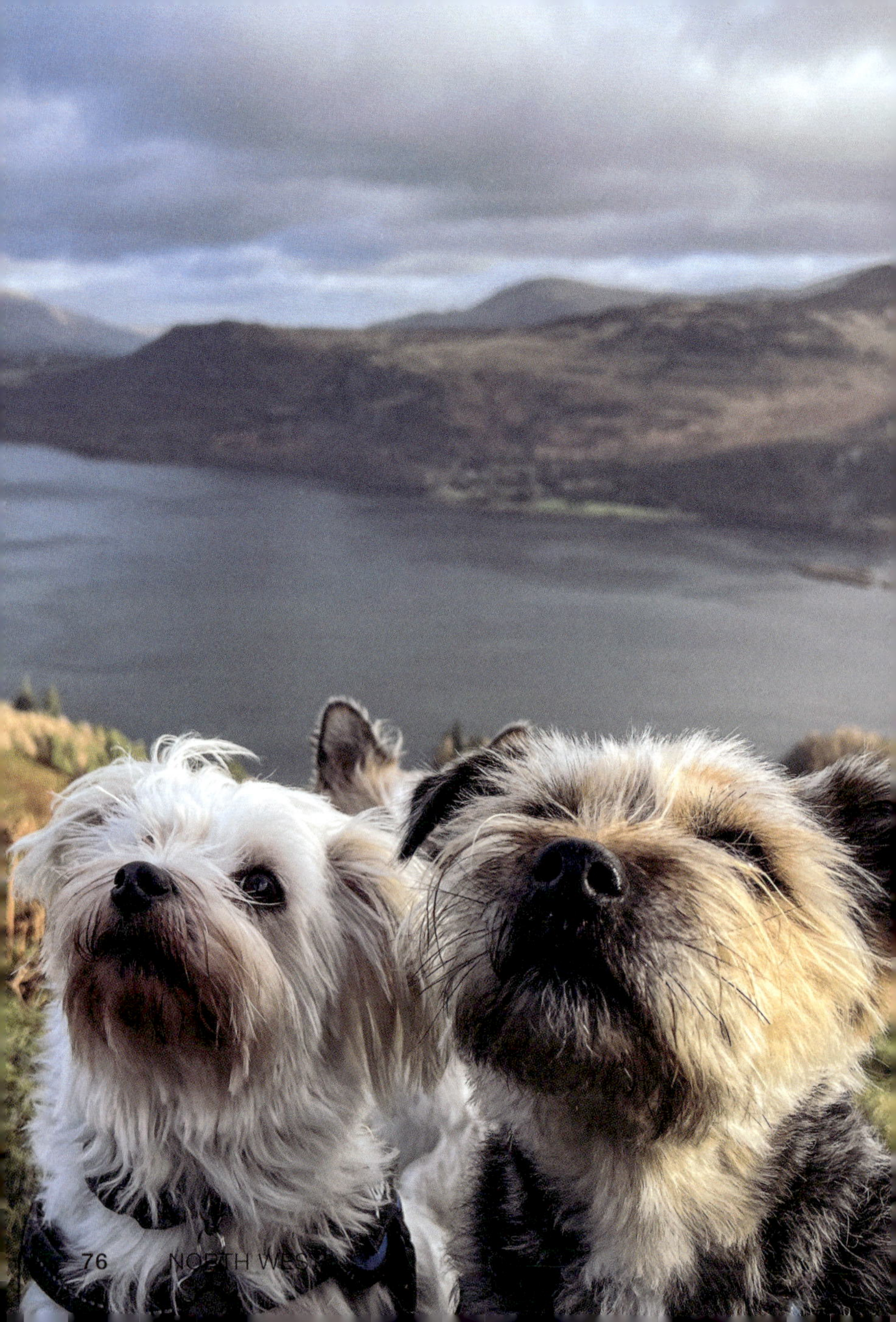

10.

Keswick

Keswick is situated on the banks of Derwentwater and is a gateway to some of the Lake District's most iconic walks, perfect for beginner and advanced fell walkers alike.

One of the most popular routes is the circular walk around Derwentwater, where you'll find gorgeous views of the lake and surrounding hills. This is a relatively easy trail, and if your dog loves swimming, it provides plenty of opportunities for them to splash in the water.

En route you'll want to make sure you don't miss the Mary Mount Hotel. This inn and pub have some of the best views you'll find to enjoy a pint or something to eat, and the garden area is filled with beautiful birds such as great tits, blue tits and goldfinches who tweet away as you soak up the surroundings.

There are also lots of moderately easy hikes that you can take right from the centre of town if you're looking to tick off some Wainwrights. Catbells is a beloved fell that offers a gentle ascent with a well-trodden path to the summit. Once at the top, you and your dog will be rewarded with views across Derwentwater and the surrounding area. It's the perfect spot to pause, catch your breath and take in the beauty of the Lake District with your dog at your side.

Another favourite is Latrigg, which has another well-marked path that leads you upwards through woods, eventually opening out to reveal a sweeping vista over Keswick. It's great for beginners as the summit makes you feel on top of the world without the exertion of a long hike.

Of course, if you're a more advanced hiker and are looking for something a bit more adventurous you'll also find Skiddaw, one of the highest fells in the Lake District; Blencathra, known for its dramatic ridges; and many more.

A short drive away there are many nearby towns that are worth visiting. I was pleasantly surprised by the Lake District's fantastically well-connected and dog-friendly bus service, meaning you can hop on and off at leisure.

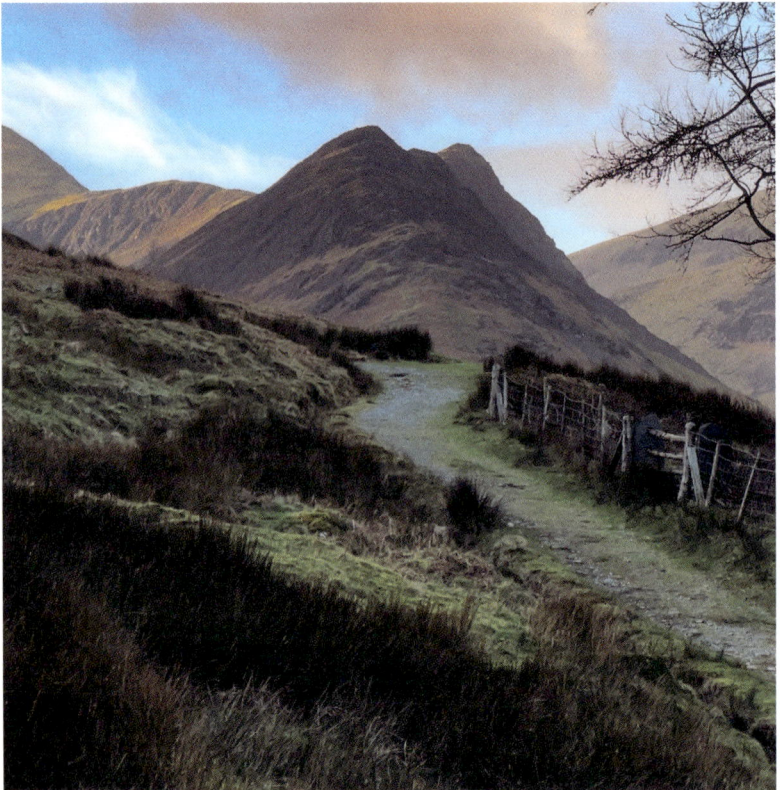

Places to explore

CATBELLS

Chapel Bridge, CA12 5TU

Rising to 451 metres above sea level, this modest yet rewarding peak is a firm favourite in the Lake District for beginners. As you climb to the summit you'll be surrounded by uninterrupted views of Derwentwater, with its shimmering waters dotted with islands and framed by the majestic fells beyond. A small amount of parking is available near Newlands Church next to Chapel Bridge, which makes a great starting point for the route.

THE PUZZLING PLACE

9 Museum Square, CA12 5DZ

If you're looking for something unique away from walking, The Puzzling Place promises a fun day out. The quirky museum is filled with optical illusions and interactive exhibits, and dogs are welcomed, allowing you to get some fantastic photos.

LATRIGG

Moot Hall, Market Square, CA12 5JR

Often referred to as Keswick's premier viewpoint, Latrigg Fell sits in a fantastic position overlooking the whole Vale of Derwent. There is an easy route up directly from the town centre, culminating in the perfect picnic spot at the summit where you'll be treated to panoramic views of the surrounding fells. This walk can be taken right from the centre of town, with a great route taking you directly from Moot Hall in the town centre.

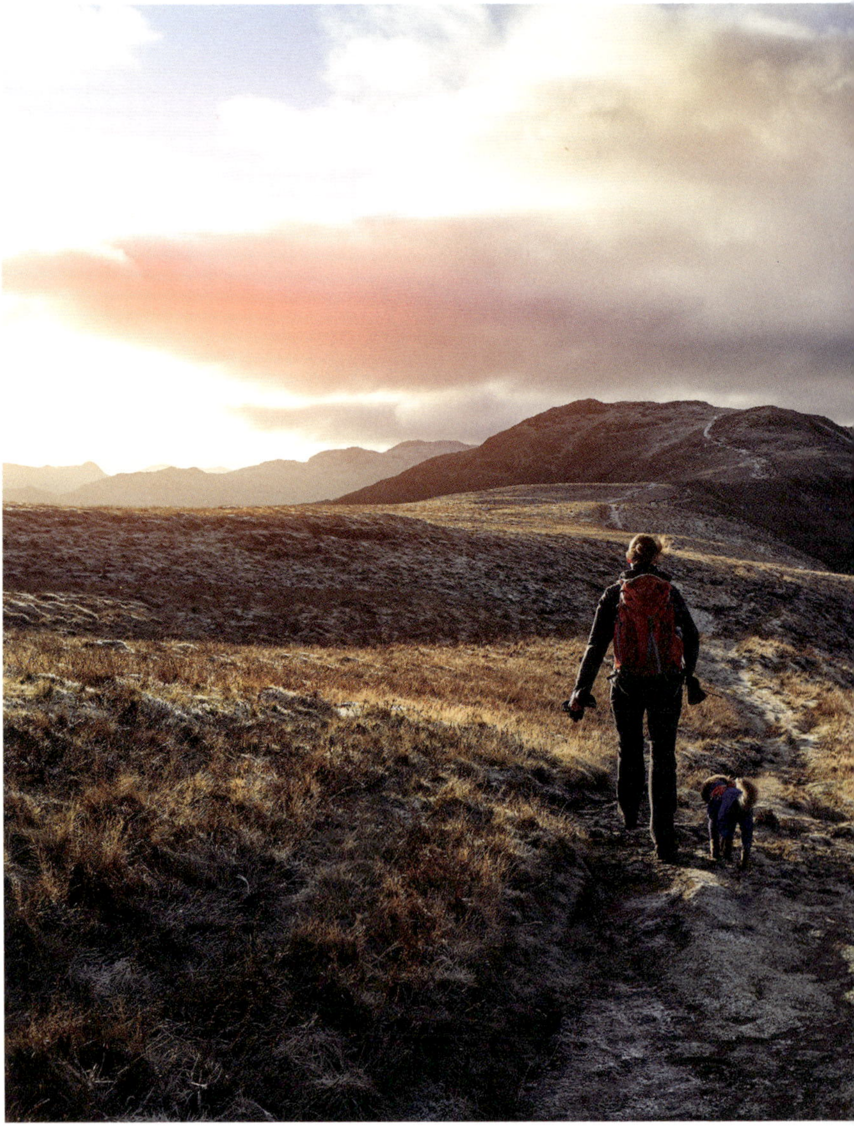

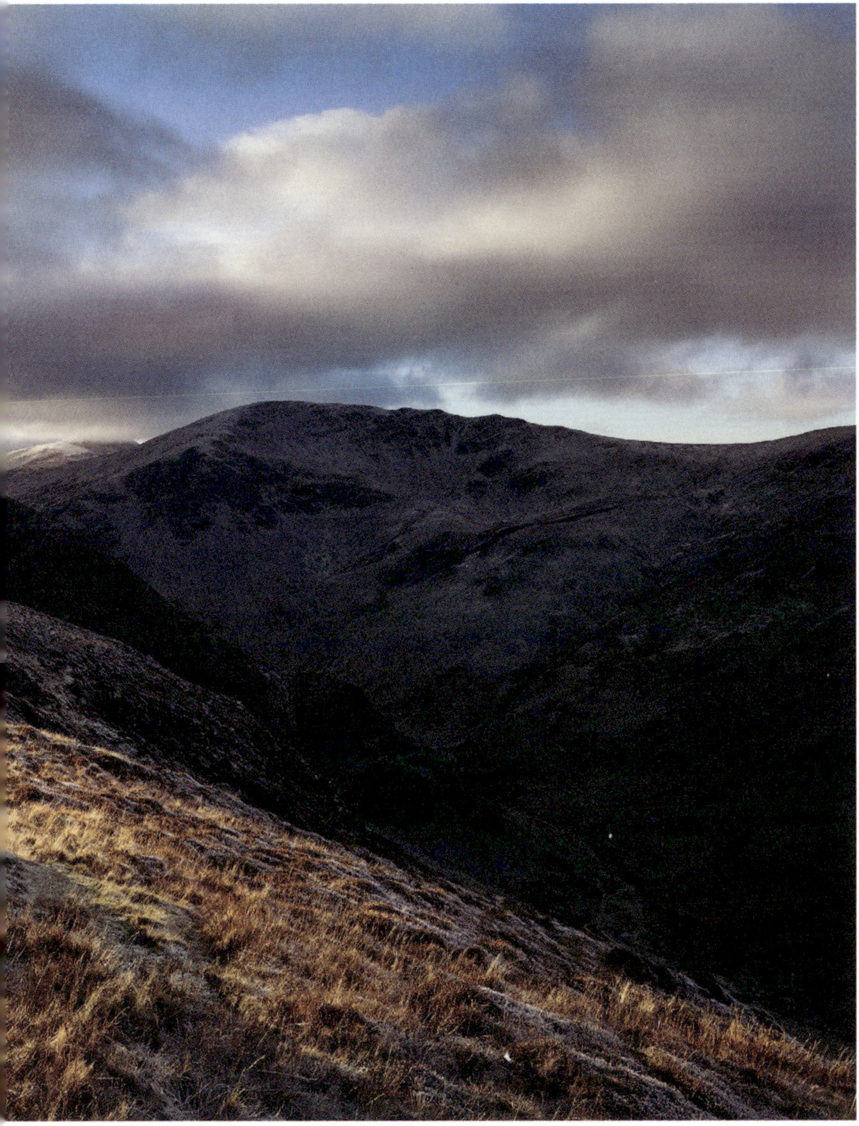

Places to eat, drink and stay 🐾🐾

THE DOG AND GUN
2 Lake Road, CA12 5BT

No visit to Keswick is complete without heading to The Dog and Gun to try their iconic Hungarian Goulash – a hearty, flavourful meal that has earned legendary status among regulars. This traditional pub is known for its dog-friendly atmosphere and relaxed and welcoming vibe, making it a fantastic choice after a day exploring the beautiful surrounding fells.

MARY MOUNT HOTEL
Borrowdale, Keswick, CA12 5UU

Perched on the edge of Derwent Water, Mary Mount Hotel is perfect for those seeking a spot to eat and drink while soaking in the spectacular views. While dogs are welcome inside and out, the outdoor terrace is particularly stunning with bird feeders attracting a vibrant array of blue tits, goldfinches and other local birds.

LODORE FALLS HOTEL AND SPA
B5289, CA12 5UX

A luxurious dog-friendly haven, Lodore Falls allows dogs in most of its bedrooms and suites. Comfy dog beds and bowls are provided, and the hotel has two dedicated dog-friendly spaces where you can relax after a day exploring the beautiful surrounding area.

THE PENN
Ambleside Road, LA23 1AQ

This boutique hotel warmly welcomes four-legged guests, providing thoughtful amenities such as cosy dog beds, water bowls and even treats on arrival. Located just a couple of minutes from both a bus and a train station, and in the centre of Windermere, makes this a great option if you don't drive.

NEW DAWN VEGAN COFFEE SHOP
Derwentwater Independent Hostel, CA12 5UP

If you're looking for a coffee fix, New Dawn serves a range of delicious coffee using beans from local roastery Podda and Wren, all from the back of their Volkswagen Fox car! You'll also find a range of sweet treats and baked goods, and it's perfectly located right on the edge of the lake, so you can enjoy your beverage with a stunning view.

CAUSEY PIKE COTTAGE
Catbells Cottages, Little Town, CA12 5TU

Part of the charming collection by Catbells Cottages, Causey Pike Cottage is located right at the base of Catbells – in fact the footpath to the summit starts from the garden! This beautifully restored cottage exudes rustic charm and is well kitted out for doggy visitors too, with a basket of towels, toys and treats.

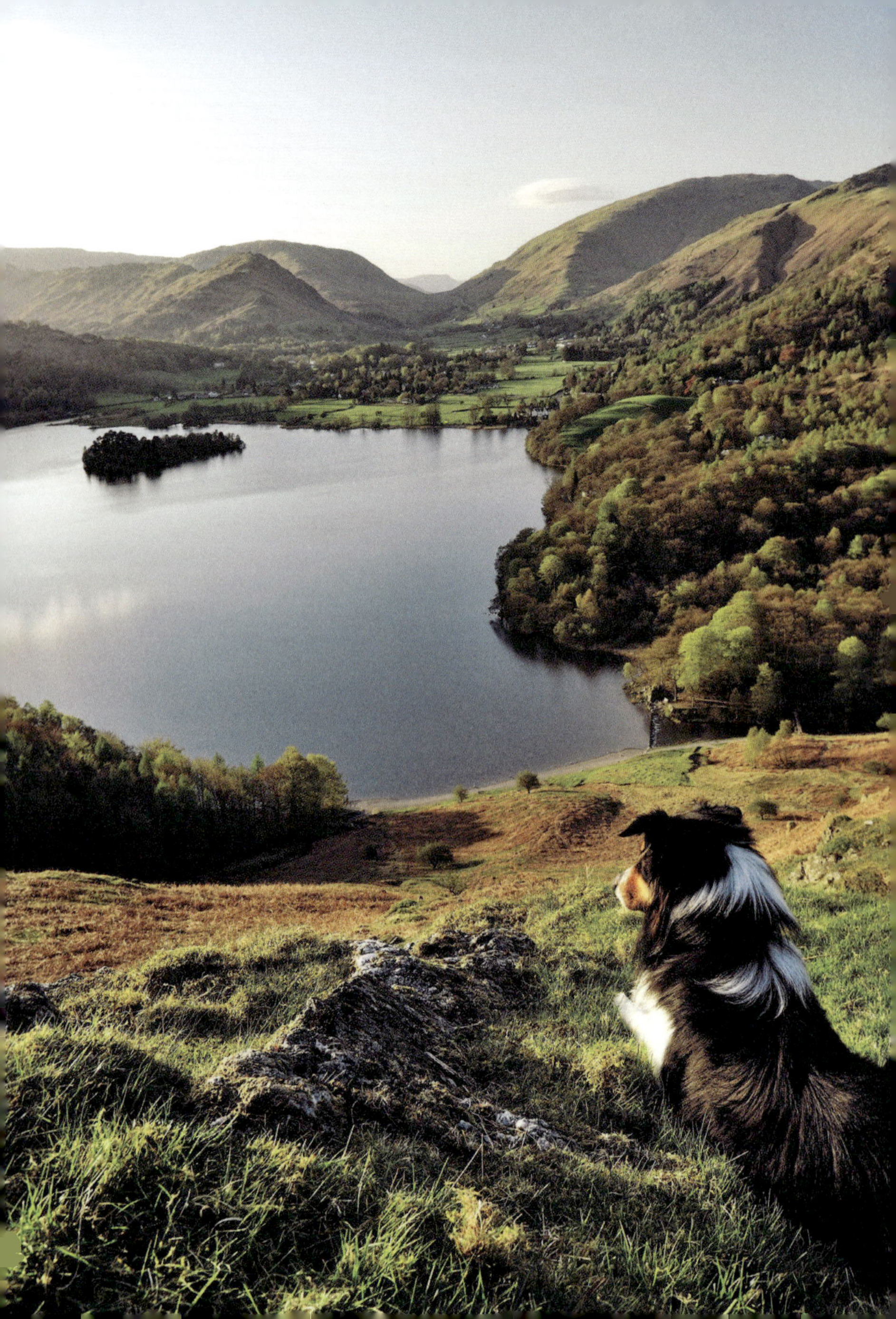

11.

Grasmere

An enchanting village renowned for its scenic walks, it's easy to see why this place and the surrounding landscapes inspired world-famous poet William Wordsworth as a haven of nature and wildlife.

If you're looking to tick off some Wainwrights there are plenty in the nearby area. From the village itself you can climb to Helm Crag – often referred to as 'The Lion and the Lamb' – which rewards adventurers with fantastic views of the Grasmere Valley, the area's rugged beauty, and the distinctive rock formations at its peak.

Another fantastic nearby walk that offers a slightly different perspective is the route to Easedale Tarn. This picturesque tarn is nestled high in the fells above Grasmere and is accessible via a well-trodden path meandering through woodlands, across streams and over gentle inclines. It's moderately challenging, but the tranquil beauty of the tarn surrounded by steep crags and rolling hills provides a rewarding destination.

One of my favourites is also the Langdale Pikes, a short drive from Grasmere. The striking peaks include Harrison Stickle, Pike of Stickle and Loft Crag. They are a challenging assent, but the sense of achievement at the summit is unmatched. At the end, enjoy a drink and a bite to eat in The Old Dungeon Ghyll, a dog-friendly pub, which is a popular haunt among walkers of the Pikes.

Nearby you'll find the larger town of Ambleside, where more walking opportunities await, or if you're looking for something a little less strenuous enjoy a cup of coffee in one of the many dog-friendly cafés, pubs and restaurants.

Drive a little further and you'll stumble across Windermere, one of the larger towns in the Lakes. From here you'll be able to take a scenic cruise across the lake where dogs are welcome aboard.

And, of course, you can't leave Grasmere without grabbing a packet of their famous gingerbread. The Grasmere Gingerbread shop, located in the heart of the village, still operates from the original cottage where the secret recipe was created. It draws quite the crowd (and for good reason, it tastes delicious!) so be prepared to queue.

Places to explore

THE GRASMERE GINGERBREAD SHOP AND ST OSWALD'S CHURCH

Church Cottage, LA22 9SW

Somewhat of an institution, a visit to the quaint Grasmere Gingerbread Shop is a must. You'll find it nestled by St Oswald's Church, where the poet William Wordsworth is buried, and while the shop itself isn't dog friendly, I'd highly recommend a wander around the tranquil church grounds as the warm comforting aroma of freshly baked gingerbread lingers in the air.

HELM CRAG (THE LION AND THE LAMB)

Keswick Road, LA22 9RE

Often called 'The Lion and the Lamb' due to its uniquely shaped rock formations, this small but dramatic fell is another rewarding yet manageable climb. Once at the top, the summit is crowned by rocky outcrops framing the captivating views across Grasmere and the surrounding area. You can either start this route in Grasmere itself, or for a shorter route there is a huge layby on the A591 at the foot of the fell.

WINDERMERE LAKE CRUISES

Promenade, Bowness-on-Windermere, Windermere, LA23 3HQ

A lake cruise is an alternative way to see the beauty of the Lake District in all its glory from the water. The cruises welcome well-behaved dogs aboard, and take you on a scenic journey across Lake Windermere – England's largest natural lake. And if you fancy yourself as the captain, Windermere Lake Cruises also offer boats you can hire yourself for the day.

Places to eat, drink and stay 🐾🐾

LAKE VIEW COUNTRY HOUSE
Lake View Drive, LA22 9TD

Tucked down a quiet lane, Lake View Country House is one of those places where dogs are not only welcomed but embraced. It's surrounded by fabulous views, with over an acre of expansive grounds for dogs to enjoy, and it's just a short walk to Grasmere village itself.

LUCIA'S COFFEE + BAKEHOUSE
College Street, LA22 9SY

Radiating a welcoming vibe from the moment you step inside, Lucia's is a cosy café adorned with wooden tables and vintage décor. Here you'll be able to enjoy amazing homemade cakes, pastries and hearty bakes, including their acclaimed sourdough bread and scrumptious brownies.

WHITE CROSS BAY HOLIDAY PARK
A591, Windermere, LA23 1LF

Set on the shores of Lake Windermere, White Cross Bay has a range of lodges and caravans that are a particularly great option for families or larger group sizes. The park has expansive grounds and a dog-friendly café, alongside an indoor pool and loads of activities to keep the family entertained.

THE GLEN ROTHAY HOTEL AND BADGER BAR
Rydal, LA22 9LR

A characterful country pub, complete with exposed beams, stone walls and a roaring fire. Dogs are welcomed here, and you can enjoy some of the best walks in the Lake District right from the door. It's the perfect place to enjoy some hearty pub grub while enjoying the historical ambience inside, or the stunning views on the terrace.

TWEEDIES BAR AND LODGE
Red Bank Road, LA22 9SW

A gem in the village, Tweedies has a warm and inviting atmosphere that is as welcoming to dogs as it is to their owners. You'll be greeted by a rustic yet cosy interior with a crackling fireplace, and the menu features hearty British pub classics alongside a wide selection of local ales and craft beers.

THE FOREST SIDE HOTEL
Keswick Road, Cumbria, LA22 9RN

Dog lovers themselves, you can expect a warm welcome at The Forest Side. Each doggy guest receives their own welcome pack, including a personalised welcome letter (how cute!), a dog bed, two dog bowls and a selection of tasty treats. What's more, the staff here have loads of knowledge about the local area and are able to suggest an abundance of walks right from the hotel door.

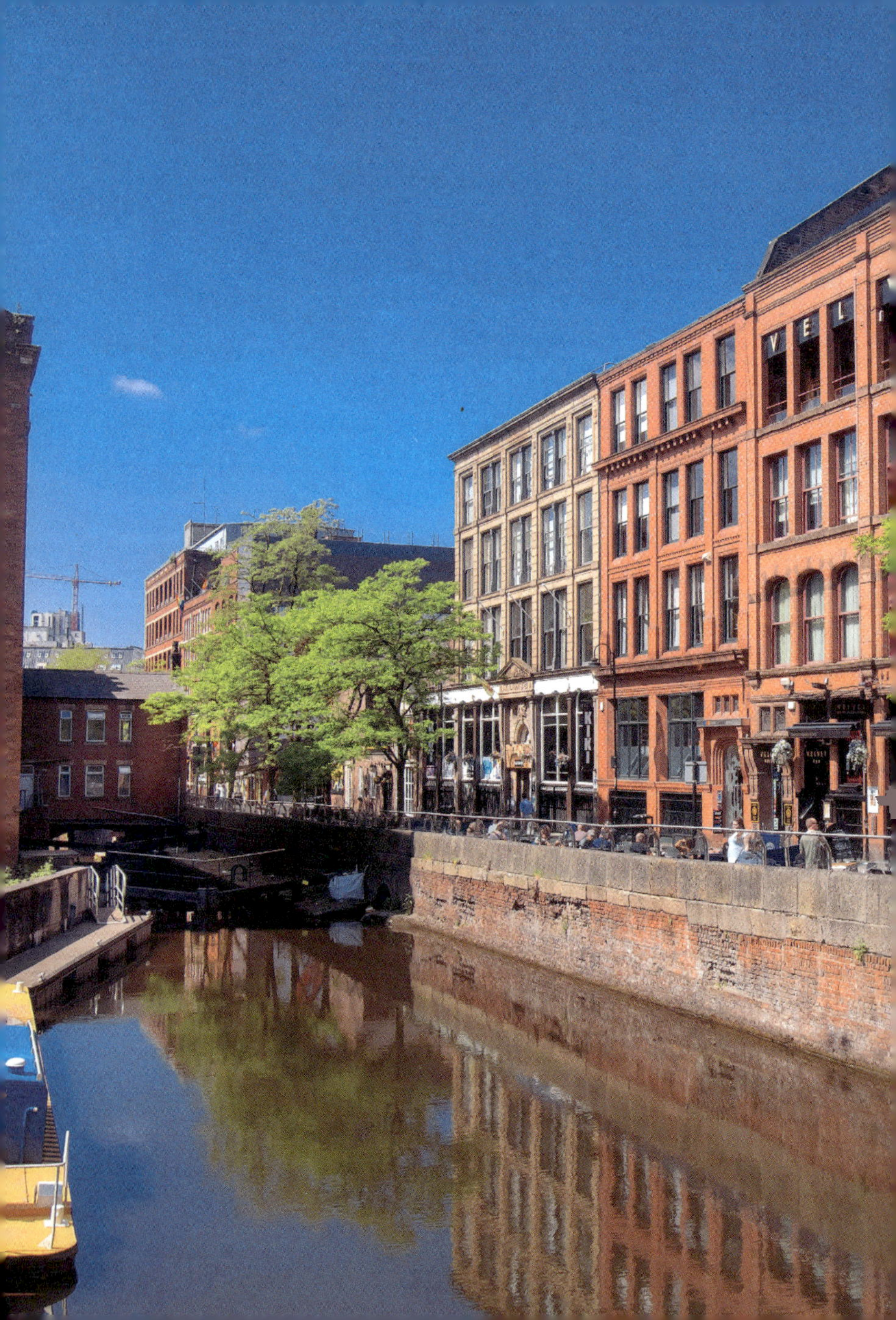

12.

Manchester

Known for its vibrant cultural scene and industrial heritage, it might come as a surprise that Manchester is also a fantastic destination for dog owners. The city has a growing array of dog-friendly activities, eateries and parks. Plus, it's on the edge of the Peak District National Park, making it an ideal spot for those who want to explore alongside their canine companions.

For those who love a good city stroll, the canals offer picturesque and historical routes that are great for getting away from the hustle and bustle of the main streets. The Rochdale Canal and Ashton Canal both provide urban backgrounds combined with tranquil waters, which make for a beautiful walking route.

One unique venue you won't want to miss is Dog Bowl, a dog-friendly bowling alley. The venue has fun, retro-inspired décor and also serves a variety of American diner-style dishes. And you can enjoy it all while your dog lounges by your side.

Another fun activity that I've not seen elsewhere is Bark N Bounce – an indoor playground designed exclusively for dogs. Located just outside the city centre it provides a safe and engaging environment where dogs can play in bouncy castles, ball pools, tunnels and more. It's truly doggy heaven!

If you're a foodie, a visit to Manchester isn't complete without heading to Mackie Mayor Food Hall in the Northern Quarter. Here you'll find a beautifully restored market hall, which is home to a variety of food vendors serving everything from wood-fired pizza to gourmet burgers. Dogs are welcomed here warmly, and the vibrant, bustling atmosphere makes it a great spot to grab lunch or dinner.

Despite being a large city, you can be surrounded by countryside in just over 30 minutes thanks to the great train network here.

A favourite spot of mine is Lyme Park, an historic estate featuring expansive grounds, formal gardens and a majestic stately home. Originally a hunting lodge owned by the Legh family for nearly 600 years, Lyme Park has grown to become one of the most visited National Trust sites in the UK.

Dogs are welcome across the park, which boasts several walking trails that vary in length and difficulty. The surrounding woodlands and moorlands provide an idyllic setting for a day out, and you can also wander into the charming nearby village of Disley to explore the quaint houses and friendly pubs.

Places to explore

DOG BOWL

57 Whitworth Street West, M1 5WW

Located in the heart of the city, this retro bowling alley is not only known for its vibrant atmosphere, but also for its dog-friendly policy. You'll find ten pin bowling alongside a retro-inspired bar and diner complete with neon lights and vintage décor.

BARK N BOUNCE

Keepers Cottage, Vicars Hall Lane, Worsley, M28 1JA

A dog's dream come true, Bark N Bounce is a dedicated indoor play area exclusively for dogs. It's designed with dogs' needs in mind, offering a variety of agility equipment, soft play zones, and even a ball pit. A real-life doggy heaven.

LYME PARK

Disley, Stockport, Cheshire East, SK12 2NR

Located just outside of Manchester, Lyme Park is a sprawling estate that was once a grand hunting ground. The majestic Lyme Hall stands proudly at the centre of the estate surrounded by breathtaking views of the Peak District. Dogs can roam freely throughout the estate's expansive trails.

Places to eat, drink and stay 🐾🐾

MACKIE MAYOR
Smithfield Market Hall, 1 Eagle Street, M4 5BU

A bustling food hall in Manchester's Northern Quarter, Mackie Mayor is a foodie's dream, and completely dog friendly too. You'll find a diverse array of food stalls that cater to all tastes, from gourmet burgers and Pad Thai to artisanal doughnuts and bao buns.

RUDY'S PIZZA
9 Cotton Street, Ancoats, M4 5BF

Literally named after the owner's dog, Rudy's is a beloved pizza spot on Manchester's food scene. Their pizzas are to die for, and they have several spots across town, so are a great option no matter which area you're exploring.

HOUSE OF ESK
6 New Union Street, Cottonfield Wharf, M4 6FQ

An eclectic café and bar, House of Esk is a great place to relax and enjoy a leisurely brunch or evening cocktail. Dogs are welcomed and there is a lovely laid-back vibe, which is a welcome oasis from the busyness of the city.

MOXY MANCHESTER CITY
8 Atkinson Street, M3 3HH

I knew this place would be cool the minute I saw that check-in was at the bar and a cocktail was provided on arrival. Moxy's is quirky and fun without compromising on comfort and a great night's sleep. They allow dogs in all their rooms and greet furry friends with bowls full of treats and even a welcome message on the mirror!

BREWDOG DOGHOUSE HOTEL
20 Fountain Street, M2 2AR

Located in the beating heart of the city, The DogHouse goes above and beyond to treat dogs like guests in their own right, with dog beds, treats and even dog-friendly craft beer. For humans, you'll find equally as many cool touches from shower beer fridges to a rooftop taco bar.

NATIVE MANCHESTER
Warehouse, Ducie Street, M1 2TP

Native Manchester is home to spacious apartments, giving you more space than a standard hotel room to relax. They provide bowls, beds and treats for your dog, and their apartments really feel like a home away from home.

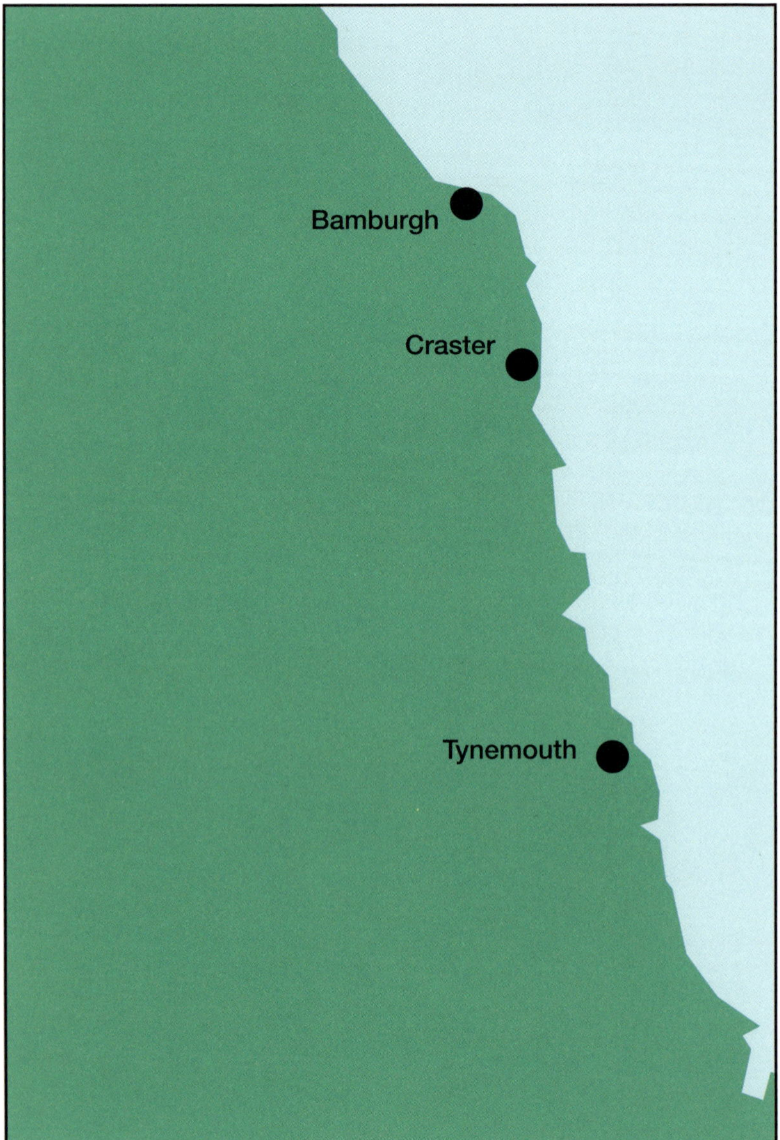
Bamburgh
Craster
Tynemouth

North East

Craster   99

Tynemouth   105

Bamburgh   113

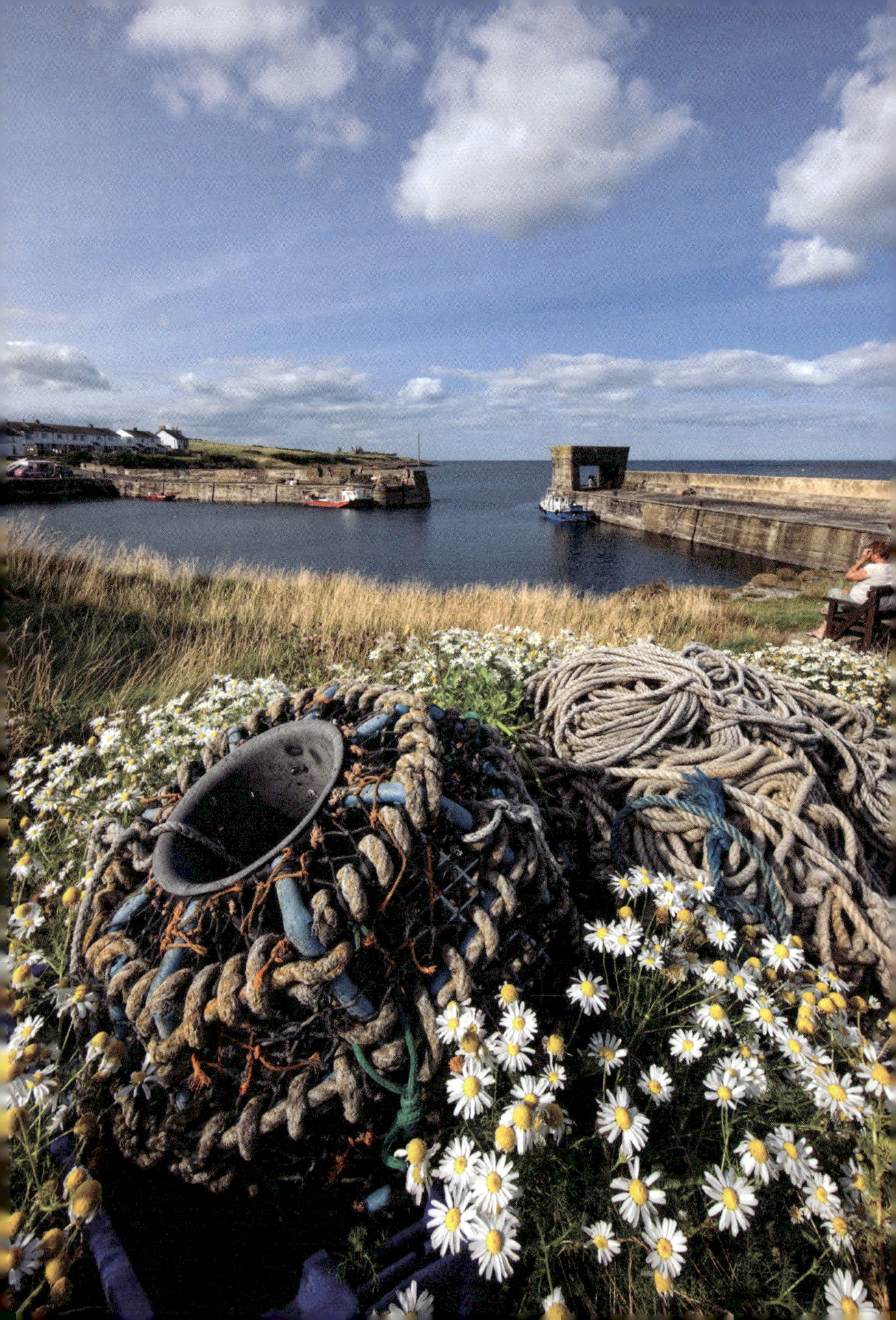

13.

Craster

Craster is a picturesque fishing village situated on the Northumberland Coast Path. Overlooked by the ruins of Dunstanburgh Castle in the distance, this is truly a majestic stretch of the English coastline.

Dunstanburgh Castle itself is a striking castle ruin perched on a rocky headland, with a history dating back to the fourteenth century. Like many English Heritage sites, it's dog friendly to visit, allowing you to explore the ancient walls and towers while your dog enjoys the open spaces. The site is steeped in history and folklore, which you can learn about on your visit, adding to the allure of the landscape.

A little further on from Dunstanburgh Castle is Embleton Bay, an extensive stretch of sandy beach that is ideal for long strolls along the shore. It's one of those places where you'll rarely see a soul and you feel that you have the entire beach to yourself.

For a longer walk, you can follow the coast path all the way up to Low Newton-by-the-Sea, another must-visit beach and breathtaking expanse of unspoiled natural beauty where, if you're lucky, you'll get the opportunity to spot seals basking on the rocks. Nestled directly on the edge of the beach is The Ship Inn, a historic pub with beautiful sea views, and the perfect place to stop for a drink or bite to eat when exploring the area.

In addition to its natural beauty, Craster boasts a rich cultural heritage. One of the first things you notice when you're in the village is the smell of smoke wafting from the traditional and world-renowned smoked kipper shop, where the Robson family have been smoking fish for generations.

Another must-visit pub located right in the heart of the village is The Jolly Fisherman. I'm not over exaggerating when I say this is one of the best meals I've ever eaten – I'm still thinking about their fish pie today! It's dog friendly in the bar area (booking ahead is highly recommended) and even has its very own dog menu.

If you're visiting in the summer months, head out to the beer garden, which overlooks the castle ruins.

Places to explore

DUNSTANBURGH CASTLE

Dunstanburgh Road, Alnwick, NE66 3TT

Striking ruins of a medieval fortress evoking tales of chivalry, battles and a rich history. The site is dog friendly, allowing dogs on leads to explore the grounds and gaze out over the dramatic landscape.

EMBLETON BAY

Dunstan Steads, NE66 3DT

Nestled along the rugged coastline, Embleton Bay is one of my favourite dog-friendly beaches in the whole of the UK. The bay is framed by sweeping golden sands and dramatic, rocky outcrops, and it's one of those places where you are unlikely to see another soul for miles, making it perfect for dogs to bound freely.

LOW NEWTON-BY-THE-SEA

Boatman's Place, Newton-by-the-Sea, NE66 3EH

Low Newton is a charming coastal village adjacent to another stunning stretch of sandy beach where soft golden grains meet the gentle surf of the North Sea, creating a perfect playground for dogs. Framed by picturesque dunes adorned with tufted grasses the beach is dog friendly year-round and has ample space for dogs to stretch their legs.

Places to eat, drink and stay 🐾🐾

THE JOLLY FISHERMAN
Haven Hill, NE66 3TR

Boasting one of the finest beer gardens in the UK, The Jolly Fisherman is a must-visit when in the area. It is the perfect warm and friendly spot to unwind after a day exploring the nearby coastline. It offers an extensive menu of delicious freshly cooked food and a dedicated doggy menu too.

THE SHIP INN
Low Newton-by-the-Sea, NE66 3EL

A quintessentially British gastropub that perfectly captures the essence of coastal village life, The Ship Inn at Low Newton is located right on the beach, making it a great spot to enjoy a drink and bite to eat after a long walk.

THE STABLE YARD
Craster Tower, NE66 3SS

Nestled in woodland at Craster Tower, The Stable Yard serves delicious homemade cakes, scones, sausage rolls, soups and sandwiches. Dog friendly throughout, it's a great stop off for lunch with a cosy fire to warm up after a walk exploring the local area.

DRIFTWOOD
Catch The Breeze Retreats, 12 West End, NE66 3TS

This coastal retreat definitely has the wow factor as soon as you walk in the door. Conveniently located in the heart of the village of Craster, I love that you can enjoy a cup of tea sat in the gorgeous window seat overlooking the harbour and watch the world go by.

THE JOINERS ARMS
B1340, High Newton-by-the-Sea, NE66 3EA

A boutique inn and gastropub that warmly welcomes dogs and their owners alike, combining rustic elegance with modern comfort. Just a short walk from the breathtaking coast, The Joiners Arms is also perfectly located for long walks on the beach.

SPRINGHILL FARM HOLIDAY ACCOMMODATION
Springhill Farm, Seahouses, NE68 7UR

Just a stone's throw from the coastal path, Springhill Farm has a range of different accommodation types to suit all budgets, from cottages and lodges, to wigwams and camping. Perfect for those who are hoping for a holiday of beach fun, you can walk from Springhill to Seahouses Beach in less than 25 minutes.

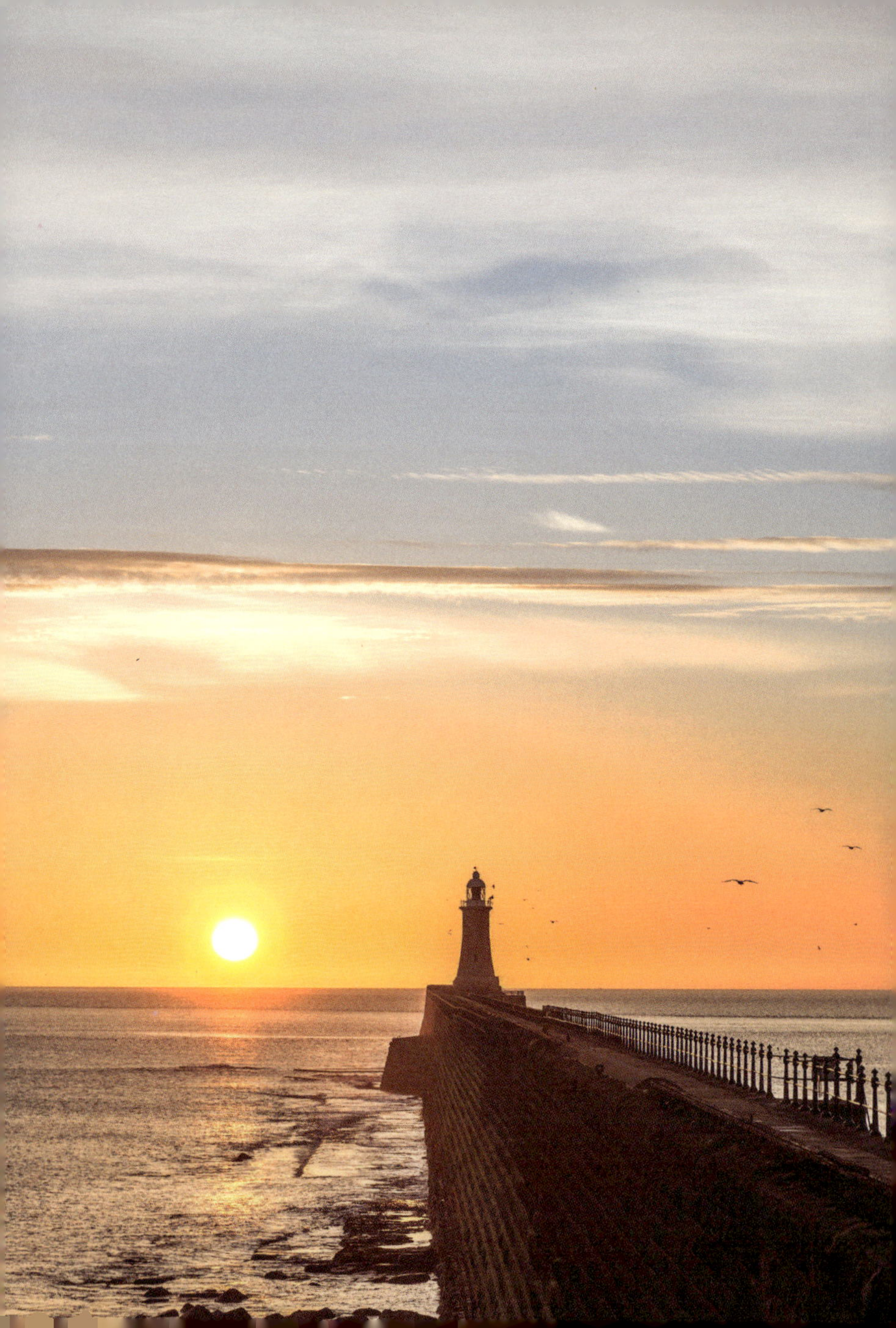

14.

Tynemouth

A charming coastal town just a short train ride from Central Newcastle, Tynemouth is an ideal destination for dog owners that feels a million miles away from the hustle and bustle of the city.

One of the standout features is the beautiful and often underrated stretch of the coastline here. Tynemouth Long Sands Beach provides wide, golden sands and gentle waves, which make a great space for dogs to run and play. Be sure to try and catch the sunrise here if you can, it is truly gorgeous.

Nearby, King Edward's Bay is also worth a visit. A smaller beach than Long Sands, it's nestled between steep cliffs, providing a more secluded and intimate setting, and is overlooked by the historic Tynemouth Priory, adding a dramatic backdrop to the tranquil shoreline.

After a brisk walk along the beach, Riley's Fish Shack is not to be missed. Located on the beach itself, Riley's offers fresh, locally sourced seafood with a view that's hard to beat. They have an ever-changing menu to reflect what's in season, and the food is delicious.

In addition to the beautiful beaches, Tynemouth itself is full of things to do and see and Tynemouth Market should definitely be top of your list. Every weekend, Tynemouth Metro station transforms into a treasure trove of local crafts, antiques, food stalls and unique finds. Dogs are welcome to stroll through the market with their owners, making it a great spot to browse for unique gifts and sample some local street food.

For those interested in history, Tynemouth Priory and Castle is a great place to learn more about the area's past. The site dates back to the seventh century, and has served various roles in its time, from a religious centre to military stronghold. The surrounding grounds are dog-friendly, and you'll be treated to stunning views over the North Sea.

If you're up for walking, I'd recommend heading up to Whitely Bay just a couple of miles away. There is a fantastic coast path between the two, where you'll find several opportunities to take in the beautiful surroundings and wildlife.

Alternatively, take the coast path in the southerly direction and you'll come to North Shields Fish Quay, a historic working fishing port. Along the front here you'll find an abundance of seafood restaurants and pubs to stop off at, many of which are dog friendly.

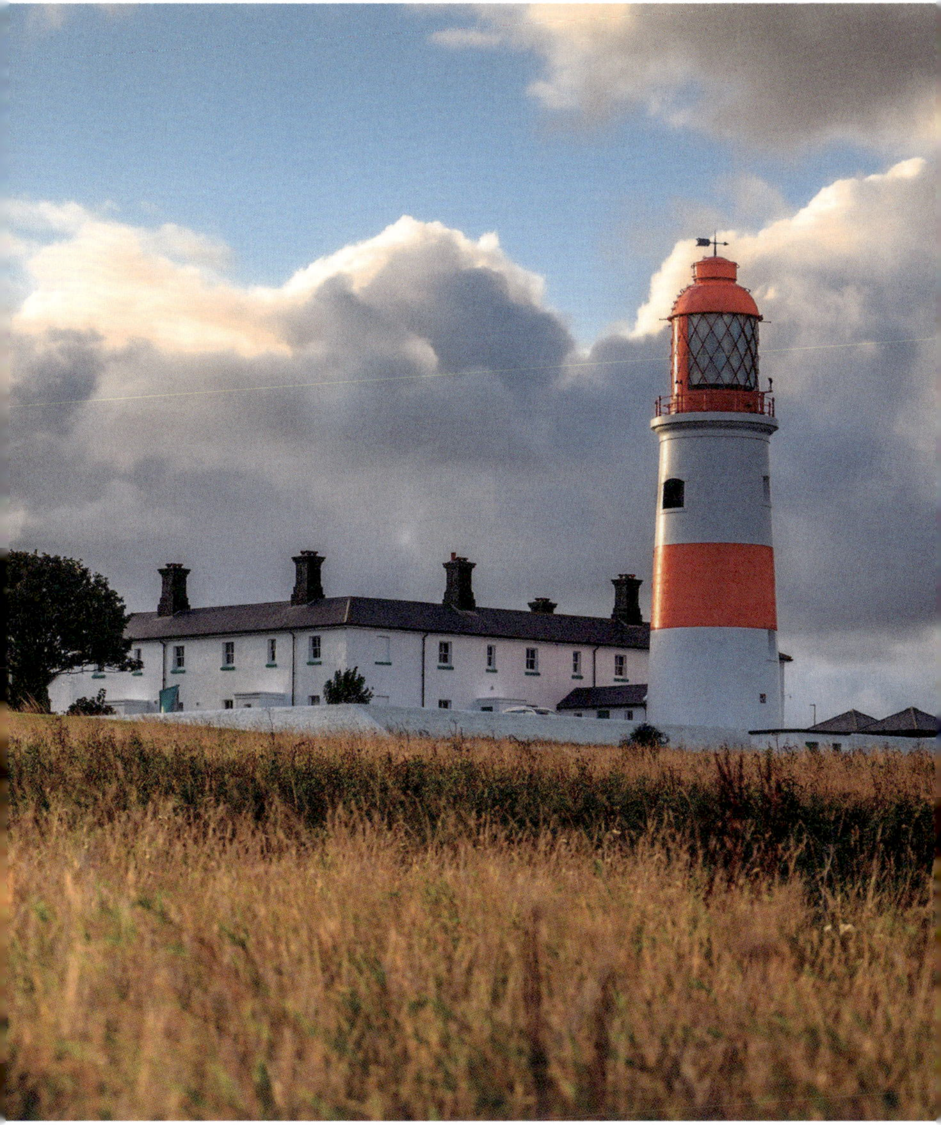

Places to explore

TYNEMOUTH MARKET
Station Terrace, North Shields, NE30 4RE

A vibrant and bustling hub of activity every weekend, Tynemouth Market has an eclectic mix of stalls offering everything from vintage clothing and antiques to artisan bakes, delicious street food and even stalls offering handmade dog treats.

LONG SANDS BEACH
Grand Parade, North Shields, NE30 4NT

A gorgeous stretch of golden sand that curves along the Northeast coast. The beach is dog friendly year-round, with only some restrictions in designated areas during the summer months, ensuring that there is always a space for dogs to enjoy the beach.

SOUTER LIGHTHOUSE AND THE LEAS
Coast Road, Whitburn, SR6 7NH

Just a short drive from Tynemouth, the unmistakable red-and-white striped Souter Lighthouse is perched dramatically on a clifftop overlooking the nature-rich coastline. It was the UK's first lighthouse designed to be lit by electricity, making it a pioneering structure of its time and an important piece of maritime history. Meanwhile, The Leas, a vast area of surrounding open grassland and coastal paths, is perfect for long leisurely walks.

Places to eat, drink and stay 🐾🐾

PLATFORM 2
Tynemouth Metro Station, NE30 4RE

Located in the historic Tynemouth Metro Station, this quirky café retains the charm of its railway origins. Dogs are warmly welcomed inside making it a great place to enjoy a coffee, light lunch or pint with your furry friend.

SEAHAM HALL HOTEL
Lord Byron's Walk, Seaham, SR7 7AG

A short drive south of Tynemouth, Seaham Hall Hotel is a luxurious dog-friendly retreat set amid a sprawling estate of 37 acres – perfect for an escape with your dog! They have dedicated Garden Suites, which boast their own outdoor spaces for dogs to roam. There's also a hot tub for you to unwind in while your dog takes a nap. Absolute bliss!

THE HEAD OF STEAM
3a The Arcade, Front Street, NE30 4BS

Head of Steam is one of those places where dogs are treated as part of the family. Inside you'll find a range of classic pub fare like juicy burgers, and fish and chips, alongside a selection of craft beers, ales, cocktails and more.

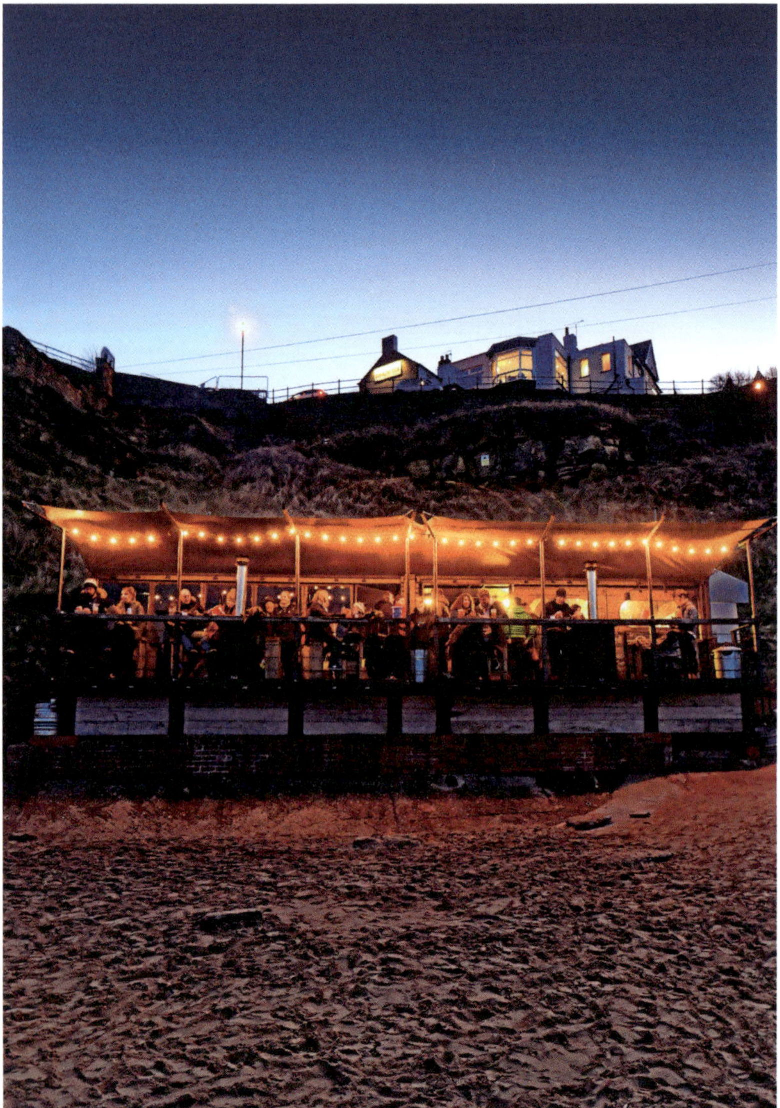

RILEY'S FISH SHACK
King Edward's Bay, NE30 4BY

This beach side gem is nestled right in the sands of King Edward's Bay and combines exceptional food with a laid-back, dog-friendly atmosphere. Housed in a converted shipping container, Riley's is a must-visit for seafood lovers.

COWRIE COTTAGE
Simpson Street, Cullercoats, NE30 4PY

Sitting proud on a row of brightly coloured cottages, Cowrie Cottage is a cosy option for two. It boasts a prime coastal location in nearby Cullercoats, making it perfectly located for exploring the nearby beaches.

TYNEMOUTH CASTLE INN
Grand Parade, NE30 4JQ

Sitting in a commanding position overlooking the sprawling Long Sands Beach, Tynemouth Castle Inn has lots of spacious and comfortable dog-friendly rooms. Located in a prime position, you'll be at the centre of the high street and next to Tynemouth Priory, perfectly situated for walking out the door straight to the coastal path to enjoy walks from the doorstep.

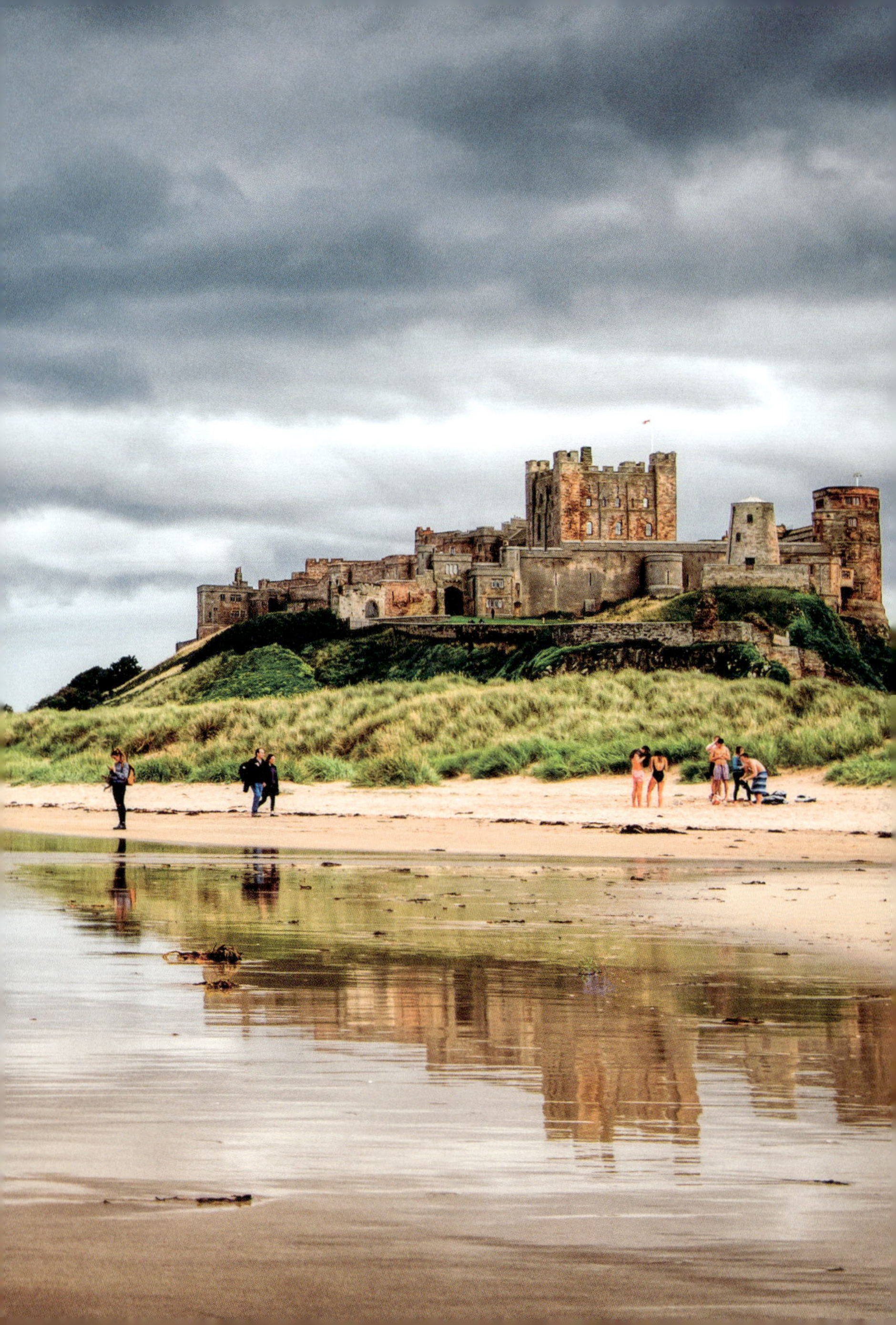

15.

Bamburgh

Bamburgh oozes both natural beauty and historic charm. Dominated by the imposing Bamburgh Castle, which stands atop a volcanic crag, the village is a haven for exploring with dogs.

Bamburgh Beach is one of the jewels in the Northumberland crown. Stretching for miles, it's dog friendly year-round, and provides plenty of space for dogs to run freely and splash in the waves.

There are some fantastic walks around here too, one of my favourites is the route north towards the village of Seahouses, which passes much of the natural beauty of the area as it meanders along the seafront with the iconic Holy Island in the distance.

Seahouses itself is a bustling fishing village with loads of dog-friendly pubs and restaurants alongside another year-round, very dog-friendly beach. It's also the gateway to the Farne Islands, which are accessible by boat trips, some of which are dog friendly. These trips offer a fantastic opportunity to see seabirds including puffins, seals and the rugged beauty of the islands.

The surrounding areas are a paradise for walkers, with a variety of trails to explore the breathtaking scenery of the Northumberland coast.

For history fanatics Bamburgh Castle is not to be missed, with dogs allowed in the grounds. It's a prominent feature on the landscape and a striking example of medieval architecture with origins that date back as far as the sixth century.

The castle has been meticulously restored and now houses a fascinating collection of artifacts. While dogs are not allowed inside the castle itself, the surrounding grounds and panoramic views enjoyed from the outer walls are well worth exploring.

The village of Bamburgh itself is a delightful place to wander with traditional stone cottages, quaint shops and welcoming pubs. I highly recommend popping into R Carter & Son, the local butchers, which serve amazing sausage rolls, and pork and stuffing rolls that will have your mouth watering. Sit and enjoy on one of the nearby benches while you take in the stunning surrounding scenery and impressive castle backdrop.

Places to explore

BAMBURGH CASTLE
Bamburgh, NE69 7DF

Perched dramatically on a rocky plateau overlooking the beautiful Northumberland coastline, Bamburgh Castle is a magnificent historic site. Once the royal capital of the ancient kingdom of Northumbria, this formidable fortress is steeped in history. Dogs are warmly welcomed in the castle's extensive outdoor areas, where they can enjoy the fresh sea breeze and spectacular views alongside their owners.

BILLY SHIELS FARNE ISLAND BOAT TRIPS
Seahouses Harbour, Seahouses, NE68 7RN

The Farne Islands are renowned for their incredible array of wildlife, and a boat trip offers a unique experience to witness the natural spectacle up close. During breeding season, the islands are teeming with thousands of seabirds, including the charming puffins, whose colourful beaks and comical waddles are enough to put a smile on anyone's face. Dogs are welcome aboard some of the Billy Shiel's trips; check the website for full details.

LINDISFARNE, HOLY ISLAND
Berwick-upon-Tweed, TD15 2SH

Lindisfarne, also known as Holy Island, is accessible via a tidal causeway, adding an element of adventure to any visit. Once on the island you and your dog can explore a variety of walking routes that wind through its diverse landscape where you'll encounter a range of wildlife, from seals lounging on the shores, to the diverse bird species that call this island home.

Places to eat, drink and stay 🐾🐾

THE LORD CREWE
Front Street, NE69 7BL

A cosy wood burner provides a welcoming retreat here on a cold winter's day, perfect after a bracing walk on the beach. Dogs are allowed in the bar area and outdoor patio where in the summer months they even serve doggy ice cream. They specialise in luxury seafood dishes, and if you're looking for a taste of the local area, I'd definitely recommend ordering the Lindisfarne oysters.

THE BAMBURGH CASTLE INN
Seahouses, NE68 7SQ

Located in Seahouses, The Bamburgh Castle Inn is a fantastic dog-friendly pub with an extensive interior, meaning you'll always find somewhere to perch. Dogs are welcome inside and out, making the outdoor seating area perfect for soaking up the sea air while enjoying a hearty pub meal and watching the boats come and go in the harbour.

The Bamburgh Castle Inn also has several dog-friendly rooms. The premium bedrooms even offer their own private balconies where you can sit and watch the boats coming and going, and if you're lucky might even glimpse dolphins, whales or seals on the horizon.

THE POTTED LOBSTER
3 Lucker Road, NE69 7BS

Another for seafood lovers, The Potted Lobster has a menu packed with fresh ingredients sourced from around the local coastline. There is a dedicated dog-friendly area here where dogs can relax and you'll always find the attentive staff give out fuss in abundance!

LYME GRASS
New Shoreston, NE69, 7AS

Located on a working farm just a few miles south of Bamburgh, you'll wake up here to the sound of cows mooing and the sight of sheep grazing in the field beyond. The cottage features an enclosed garden making it easy to relax with a secure space for dogs to play freely.

CUTHBERT COTTAGE
The Haven, Beadnell, Chathill, NE67 5DB

Just a short stroll from Beadnell Bay, Cuthbert Cottage is an excellent base for exploring the coastline. There is a small, enclosed patio area and inside traditional features are combined with modern furnishings for a contemporary feel. Best of all you're just a minutes' walk from not one but two dog-friendly pubs.

Robin Hood's Bay

York

Harrogate

Yorkshire

York	121
Robin Hood's Bay	127
Harrogate	133

MONK BAR CHOCOLATIERS
Handmade Artisan Chocolates
W. HAMOND
S

16.

York

This ancient city has a tapestry of things to see and do for both humans and dogs alike. From cobbled streets to sprawling green spaces, York has many facets and beautiful walking routes.

The Shambles is, of course, a must-see. The famously narrow and picturesque street is brimming with historic charm accentuated by its Tudor-style buildings and quaint shops. The street gets extremely busy, so I recommend heading there in the early morning or later in the evening when it's less crowded to fully enjoy the atmosphere.

If you're looking to escape the crowds, a little outside the city centre you'll find Breezy Knees Gardens, known for its beautifully curated flowerbeds and peaceful setting. You'll be able to leisurely meander through the award-winning vibrant seasonal displays covering over 20 acres with 10,000 different varieties of plants.

There are also several walks you can take in the area, the River Ouse providing a particularly scenic route. The paths are perfect for a stroll with views of the water and the city's historic buildings as it winds through the heart of the city. There are plenty of places to stop en route to enjoy a picnic or simply take in the views.

If you'd rather travel in style there are a range of dog-friendly cruises you can also take down the river, a fantastic way to see York's many architectural highlights.

To find out more about the history of the city I'd recommend taking a self-guided tour. You can download loads for free online, which take in some fantastic

sights, such as Clifford's Tower, the city walls, York Minster and the Jorvik Viking Centre and they are great for getting your bearings. Plus, you can go at your speed making it perfect when travelling with dogs.

A little outside the centre you'll find Knavesmire, one of York's ancient commons. A large and historic open space next to York Racecourse, it's a fantastic spot for dog walks with extensive park land and open fields, and boasts unobstructed views of the surrounding landscape, including distant views of York Minster and the city skyline.

Of course, the gorgeous Yorkshire Dales, North York Moors and Wolds are right on the doorstep, so once you've explored all there is to see in the city itself you won't be stuck for things to do.

Places to explore

SELF-GUIDED CITY TOUR

A self-guided tour is one of the best ways to see York at your own pace. There are loads of free ones online that take you around the main city attractions and tell you information about the history of the medieval streets here, such as www.visityork.org.

DALBY FOREST

Dalby Forest Drive, Low Dalby, Pickering, YO18 7LT

Dalby Forest is a fantastic destination with a diverse range of walking paths and trails in the heart of the North York Moors. Keep your eyes peeled along the way for sculptures that are dotted throughout the woods, and the abundance of internationally recognised wildlife, such as rare pine martins and around half of England's red squirrel population that call this place home. It's also a designated Dark Sky Discovery Site, which means if you head here after the sun goes down you'll get a chance to see the Milky Way.

SHAMBLES

York, YO1 7LZ

One of York's most iconic and picturesque streets, the Shambles is a narrow cobblestone lane lined with overhanging timber-framed buildings dating back to the fourteenth century, and visiting is the perfect way to soak up York's medieval charm. It's home to a variety of independent shops, cafés and boutiques, but be sure to visit early or late in the day to avoid the crowds.

Places to eat, drink and stay 🐾🐾

THE WHIPPET INN
15 North Street, YO1 6JD

A hidden gem, The Whippet Inn can be found tucked away down a back street. Blink and you'll miss it. Filled with unusual décor and a menu full of quality and creative food, if you're looking for a special meal, The Whippet is a great option. Dogs are welcome in their front dining room.

THE IRISHMAN'S COTTAGE
Dovecote Barns, Manor Farm, Kelfield, YO19 6RG

A romantic cottage for two, The Irishman's Cottage is the perfect place to wind down after a busy day exploring York. It features a log-burning stove (an essential in my opinion!) and original features, plus an outdoor patio for relaxing in the summer.

THE TALBOT MALTON
Yorkersgate, Malton, YO17 7AJ

Located away from the city in the market town of Malton, The Talbot Malton is a historic coaching inn, which features spacious dog-friendly rooms. Best of all there are loads of dog walks that leave straight from the hotel door whether you're looking for an amble around town, or a stroll along the river.

PARTISAN
112 Micklegate, YO1 6JX

This vibrant café has a relaxed bohemian vibe and serves breakfast, brunch, lunch and afternoon tea, including an extensive vegan menu. Inside you'll be able to grab a quality coffee among its gorgeous interiors where they also regularly host art exhibitions.

THE MILNER YORK
Station Road, YO24 1AA

Blending the grandeur of late-Victorian architecture with the comforts of modern travel, The Milner York (previously the Principal York) is the perfect base for four-legged friends to explore this historic city. They even offer a special doggy package, which includes welcome treats, poo bags and a dog bed.

HOUSE OF THE TREMBLING MADNESS
48 Stonegate, YO1 8AS

If you're a lover of craft beer you'll want to add House of the Trembling Madness to your York to-do list. Located on Stonegate, one of York's most historic streets, this quirky venue is set within a twelfth-century building that once served as a medieval hall. Food is served all day long and dogs are welcome throughout.

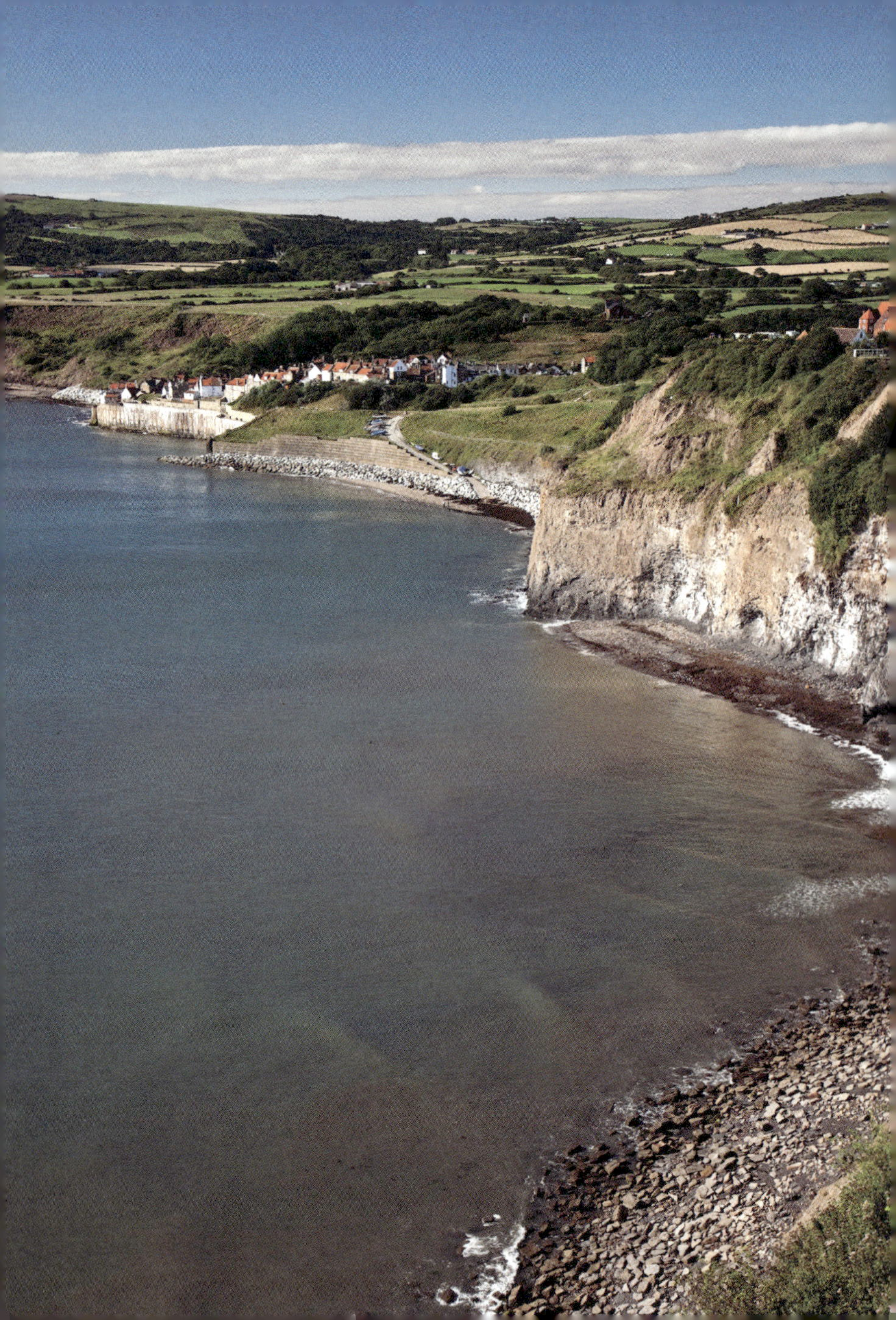

17.

Robin Hood's Bay

Robin Hood's Bay is a charming coastal village, located between Whitby and Scarborough, and on the eastern end of Wainwright's Coast-to-Coast path. Set between steep cliffs and the North Sea, the village exudes character and is known for its quaint narrow and cobbled streets that twist and turn down to the sea.

It's steeped in history, with legends of smuggling and piracy, and so-called because it's thought Robin Hood himself took refuge here while on the run. There are even underground passages underneath some of the old houses in the village, which lead down to the beach.

The beach here is dog friendly year-round and when the tide is out there is a sweeping expanse of sand to run along backed by craggy cliffs. Nicknamed the Dinosaur Coast, the beach is popular with fossil hunters – keep a look out for ammonites, belemnites and footprints from the Cretaceous and Jurassic periods!

One of the main attractions here is the opportunity to take advantage of the beautiful walks that you can take in the local area. The Cleveland Way is one I particularly recommend. It follows a cliff-top path looking out over beautiful bays and beaches below, all the way to Whitby.

For a more leisurely route the Cinder Track is a disused railway line turned footpath with a gentler incline that runs all the way from Scarborough to Whitby taking in rolling hills, farmland and the sea views that make this part of the Yorkshire coast so special.

In addition to its natural beauty, Robin Hood's Bay has a few charming independent shops, cafés and pubs that are worth a visit. Many are dog friendly and welcome furry friends with open arms.

Whether you walk or drive there, while in the area a visit to Whitby is a must. Famous for its connection to Bram Stocker's *Dracula*, Whitby has a range of dog-friendly things to see and do.

Explore the eerie remains of Whitby Abbey, taking in the incredible views across the rooftops before heading down the 199 steps to the old town known for its unique shops.

Make sure you stop off at Whitby Glass Ltd, where you can buy one of the small hand-made glass 'Lucky Ducks' said to bring luck to those who carry them and sold by Whitby Glass for over 50 years as an iconic souvenir.

A little further down the coast you'll also find Scarborough, another classically British seaside town with both natural beauty and historic charm. One of the town's unique highlights is the Scarborough Central Tramway, a funicular railway that connects the town's bustling promenade with the upper town. It's a great way to explore the town, and is dog-friendly too.

Places to explore

WHITBY ABBEY

Abbey Lane, YO22 4JT

This impressive ruin of a seventh-century monastery offers views across the bay and surrounding coastline. Dogs are allowed in the abbey grounds on leads, making it a great spot to explore. You'll also be able to find out more about the abbey's famous link to the classic novel *Dracula*, which adds an intriguing layer to its already captivating history.

THE CINDER TRACK

Southend Gardens, YO21 1JY

Following the path of the former Scarborough to Whitby railway line, this 21-mile trail is a perfect mix of coastal views, lush countryside and seaside villages. You can pick up the trail at Robin Hood's Bay and walk towards Whitby on a 6-mile route, which winds its way along the North Yorkshire Coast.

CLEVELAND WAY

This national trail stretches along the dramatic cliffs of the North York Moors, with fantastic views of the North Sea and the historic town of Whitby. Running for 109 miles all the way from Helmsley to the coastal town of Filey, you can pick up a significant portion of this stunning route from Whitby, which offers a scenic and manageable segment of dramatic coastal cliffs and countryside to explore.

Places to eat, drink and stay 🐾🐾

THE BAY HOTEL
Whitby, YO22 4SJ

Located right by the beach, The Bay Hotel has spectacular views over the bay and beach at the bottom of the village, where the cobbled streets meet the sea. You'll be able to enjoy a beer while watching tourists and villagers alike go about their days, or if the weather isn't on your side dogs are also welcomed inside too.

SMUGGLERS ALE HOUSE
Whitby, YO22 4SJ

Small and intimate, the Smugglers Ale House exudes old-world charm. It's well known for its selection of local craft beers and ales, carefully curated to showcase the best of Yorkshire's brewing heritage and dogs are welcomed inside.

WHITBY BREWERY TAP
East Cliff, YO22 4JR

Perched near the famous Whitby Abbey, this rustic taproom is housed in a beautifully restored barn and dogs are welcome inside and out. Alongside an extensive beer list, you'll find a range of tasty freshly prepared stone-baked pizzas.

BIKE AND BOOT SCARBOROUGH
Cliff Bridge Terrace, YO11 2HA

If you're looking for quirky and right on the beach, check out the Bike and Boot in Scarborough. The vibrant hotel warmly welcomes dogs, and they even have an on-site cinema you can both relax in! It's only a few minutes' walk from Scarborough's dog-friendly beach too, and they can get sandy to their heart's content as they also have their own dog wash in the hotel.

LENWOOD
Robin Hood's Bay, YO22 4SU

A cosy sandstone cottage in the heart of the Bay, Lenwood is brightly decorated and certainly has the olde worlde feel. The views from the top floors are something else, gazing over the orange tiled roof tops across to the sea and headland. Up to two dogs are welcome.

SUNNYSIDE COTTAGE
Whitby, YO22 4SR

A traditional fisherman's cottage in the lower village, Sunnyside is located just a minute away from the beach and is the perfect place to experience Robin Hood's Bay. It's super dog friendly here, with dogs allowed on the furniture, a doggy toy box and spare leads too.

18.

Harrogate

Known for its exquisite gardens, historic architecture and vibrant culture, Harrogate is a gateway to the Yorkshire Dales and a gorgeous Victorian spa town.

In the centre of town you'll find the famous Valley Gardens, a beautiful 17-acre park with a range of formal flower beds, tranquil wooded areas and wide open spaces that make it perfect for exploring with your dog. The Japanese Garden is particularly enchanting, with ornate bridges and streams that trickle by.

If you're after a slightly longer walk, you'll find the spectacular landscapes of the Yorkshire Dales just a short drive away. There are a diverse range of trails to be found here, from gentle riverside ambles to more challenging hikes across rolling hills and rugged moorlands.

One of my favourites is the circular walk from Grassington, taking you along the River Wharfe and through the neighbouring villages. It's well-marked and mostly flat with plenty of opportunities for your dog to have a paddle in the river.

For a more strenuous outing, the hike to Malham Cove is not to be missed. The path to the top of the cove includes a section of steep stone steps, but the effort is well worth it for the breathtaking vistas over the surrounding landscape.

Nearby Janet's Foss is also a fantastic walk – a beautiful waterfall tucked away in the enchanting woodlands. The secluded spot is named after a local fairy queen who, according to legend, once lived in the cave behind the waterfall. It's one of those places where you won't be able to put your camera down as the cascade of water tumbles over a limestone outcrop into an emerald pool below.

Harrogate itself is a very dog-friendly town, with many of the cafés, tea rooms, pubs and shops all allowing dogs inside. One of the standout locations is the Montpellier Quarter, known for its boutique shops and quaint cafés where you'll be able to spot Georgian and Victorian architecture.

And you can't visit Harrogate without stopping for afternoon tea. The famous Betty's Tea Room, allows dogs in the outdoor seating area, and there are several others that are dog friendly inside and out.

The town also holds a range of markets, which are well worth checking out, including the famous Farmers' Market held regularly in the town centre, where you can pick up a variety of local produce and sample street food.

Places to explore

VALLEY GARDENS

Valley Drive, HG1 2SZ

A beautifully landscaped park, Valley Gardens is perfect for a leisurely dog-friendly walk. Tucked away in the heart of Harrogate, this 17-acre garden is filled with vibrant flower beds, lush lawns, and winding paths that offer plenty of space for dogs to explore.

MALHAM COVE

Malham, Skipton, BD23 4DJ

Malham Cove is a breathtaking limestone formation. The 80-metre high cliff face is the highlight of the walk, with a natural amphitheatre of towering rock, which makes for an awe-inspiring sight. The route is well marked and passes through picturesque countryside, babbling streams and ancient stone walls. At the top you'll be rewarded with panoramic views of the surrounding Yorkshire Dales, with its vast rolling hills and dramatic landscapes.

JANET'S FOSS

Malham, Skipton, BD23 4DL

This woodland waterfall is not to be missed. The trail to the waterfall winds through ancient woodlands, where moss-covered trees and the sound of birdsong create an enchanting atmosphere that feels like something out of a fairytale. In fact, the area is steeped in local folklore, with tales of Janet, a fairy queen, said to live in a nearby cave.

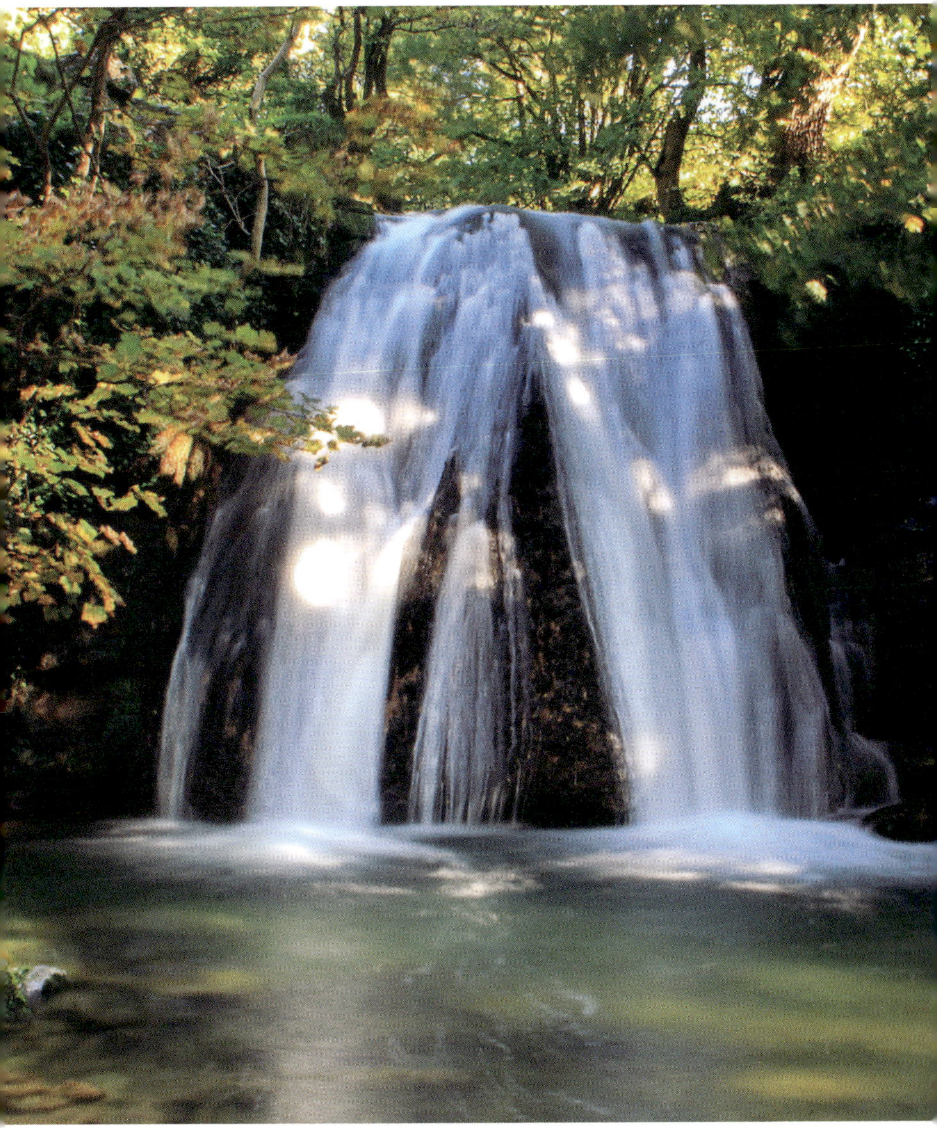

Places to eat, drink and stay 🐾🐾

HARROGATE TAP
Harrogate Station, Station Parade, HG1 1TE

A real-ale drinkers paradise serving a range of local ales and over 130 different beers. The bar is located within the only remaining part of the original Harrogate train station, so you'll find it full of history with lots of original features such as wall-to-ceiling woodwork and an open fire.

LOVE BROWNIES
28 Montpellier Parade, HG1 2TG

If you've got a sweet tooth, Love Brownies has to be on your list of places to visit in Harrogate. All handmade in the heart of the Yorkshire Dales they are decadent, gooey and just as brownies should be. They also serve a range of food and drink here and are super dog friendly, even stocking doggy ice cream.

BALTZERSEN'S
22A Oxford Street, HG1 1PU

With roots in Scandinavian cuisine, Baltzersen's is brimming with a hygge vibe. You'll find hordes of delicious freshly baked goods on offer here alongside great breakfast, brunch and lunch menus. Dogs are welcome inside and out.

THE CROWN HOTEL
Crown Place, HG1 2RZ

Dogs receive a royal welcome at The Crown with the 'Ultimate Dog Package', which includes a box of delicious snacks, a new toy and other necessities to 'pawfect' their stay. With a history dating back over 300 years, The Crown is in an enviable location, just moments from Harrogate's most popular sites, Montpellier Gardens and Valley Gardens, which are perfect for beautiful walks in this historic Victorian spa town.

THE OLD SWAN
Swan Road, HG1 2SR

Originally an eighteenth-century coaching inn, The Old Swan Hotel has a welcoming atmosphere for both guests and their furry companions. It oozes Victorian opulence, and sits in picturesque gardens, providing plenty of space for leisurely walks.

HOW STEAN GORGE CHALET LODGES
How Stean Gorge, Lofthouse, HG3 5SF

Located in the stunning How Stean Gorge, these lodges are perfectly placed for outdoor adventures, while being a stone's throw from Harrogate itself. You'll find them equipped with hot tubs, log burners, BBQs and even fire pits. Be sure to check out the Stean Gorge Café, where you'll find floor-to-ceiling glass walls and a partial glass floor overhanging the gorge below.

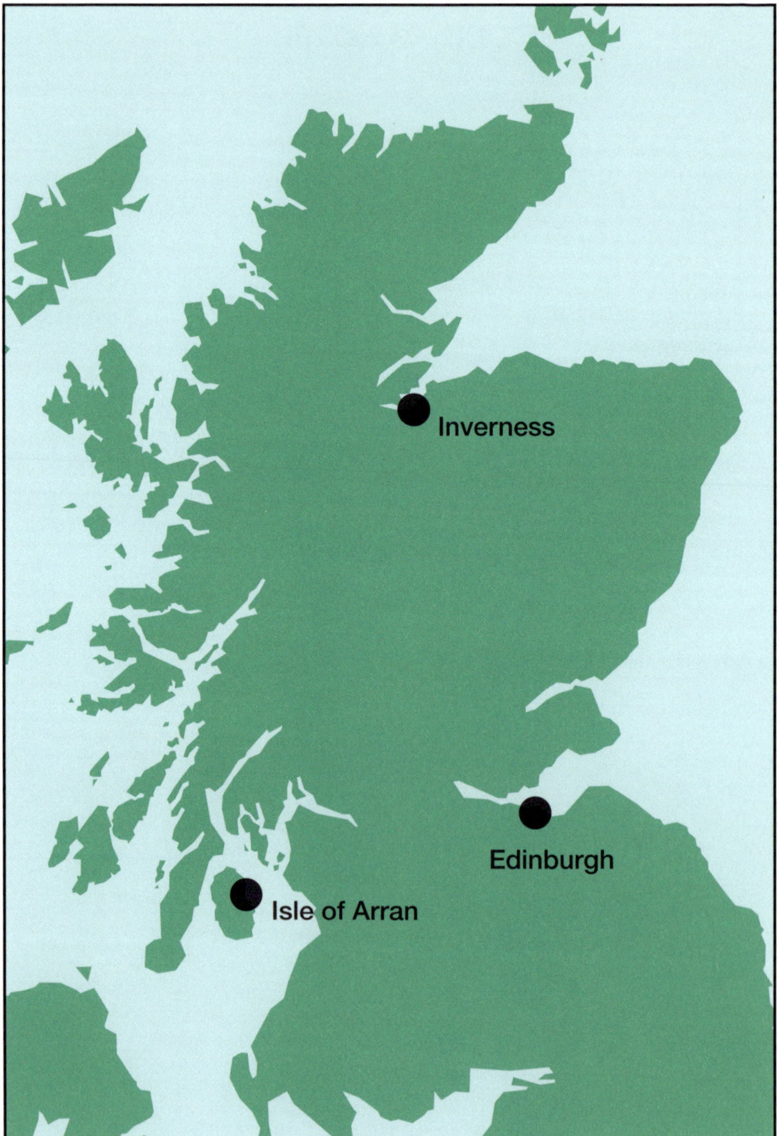
Inverness
Edinburgh
Isle of Arran

Scotland

Edinburgh	143
Isle of Arran	149
Inverness	155

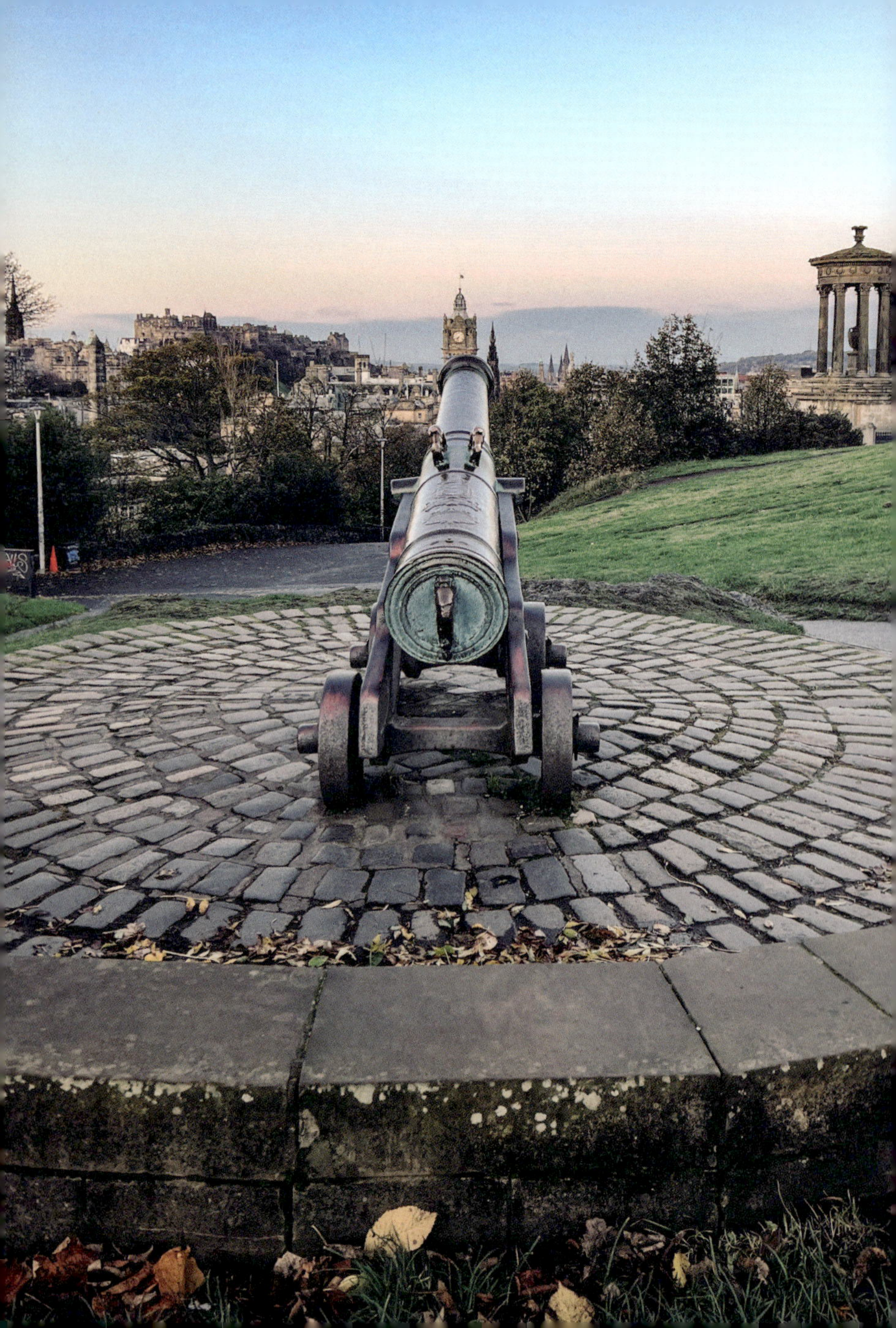

19.

Edinburgh

From lush green parks and scenic viewpoints to charming streets and dog-friendly museums, Edinburgh is a city that has it all for dog owners.

One of the highlights, and the thing that surprised me most about Edinburgh, is the number of outdoor spaces. Most famous is Arthur's Seat, the ancient volcano that rises dramatically from Holyrood Park. The climb to the summit is invigorating and offers panoramic views across the city and beyond.

Another iconic viewpoint is Calton Hill. It is particularly beautiful at sunrise as you look across to the sea. The gentle ascent is manageable for most dogs and the early morning light casts a magical glow over the cityscape.

For more relaxed walks the city also boasts numerous parks including Princes Street Gardens located in the heart of Edinburgh. It's a great spot for a leisurely stroll among historical monuments and well-manicured lawns and gardens with the castle looming over.

A great way to see all the sights this amazing city has to offer is by taking a hop on-hop off sight-seeing bus tour, some of which are dog friendly. It allows you to visit major attractions at your own pace and the open-top buses allow you to experience a unique vantage point.

Be sure not to miss Greyfriars Bobby, a beloved figure in Edinburgh's history and folklore, symbolising the loyalty and devotion of dogs. This Skye Terrier famously spent 14 years guarding his owner's grave after his death and his story has become a poignant part of Edinburgh's heritage ever since.

Today a statue of Bobby stands near to the entrance of Greyfriars Kirkyard where dog lovers often stop to pay tribute to the faithful pup. It serves as a touching reminder of the deep bond we share with our canine companions and is a must-see for anyone exploring Edinburgh with their dog.

If you're looking to head out to the coast, there are several dog-friendly beaches just a short trip away. Portobello beach is one of the best in the region and ideal for a relaxed walk. It has a lovely sandy stretch that is perfect for exerting some energy and is a fantastic spot to escape the hustle and bustle of the city.

Places to explore

ARTHUR'S SEAT

Queen's Drive, Holyrood Park, EH8 8HG

This ancient volcano rises above the city and is a rugged yet accessible trail that feels a million miles away from a capital city. Part of Holyrood Park, the path to the summit takes you through diverse terrain, with plenty of opportunities for dogs to explore the wide-open spaces. Once at the top you and your dog can enjoy sweeping views of Edinburgh, the Firth of the Forth and the surrounding coast and countryside.

PRINCES STREET GARDENS

Princes Street, EH2 2HG

A beautiful oasis in the heart of the city, Princes Street Gardens is behind bustling Princes Street and the towering Edinburgh Castle above. The gardens are well maintained, with a meandering route of tree-lined paths and flower beds that include seasonal displays. My favourite time to visit here is in the autumn when the trees turn a fantastic shade of yellow and red and it is particularly beautiful at sunset.

PORTOBELLO BEACH

Promenade, Portobello, EH15 2DX

Located just a few miles from Edinburgh's city centre, Portobello Beach has an expansive shoreline that stretches for miles, with the gentle waves of the Firth of Forth estuary providing a peaceful soundtrack as you stroll along the water's edge. Your dog will love the freedom to run and splash in the shallow surf, especially during low tide when the beach extends even further.

Places to eat, drink and stay 🐾🐾

EDINBURGH STREET FOOD
Leith Street, EH1 3AU

This bustling market is packed full of a diverse range of food stalls, serving everything from pizza to global street-food delicacies. The seating area is open and relaxed, and dogs are welcome to join their owners and enjoy the scent of deliciousness wafting in the air.

HOLYROOD 9A
9a Holyrood Road, EH8 8AE

You know it's good here, because its permanently busy, and the atmosphere is buzzing despite being a little off the beaten track. You'll find world-class burgers with a range of different options and a friendly doggy welcome with treats and fuss in abundance. Booking ahead is highly advised.

THE CITY CAFÉ
19 Blair Street, EH1 1QR

The City Café has an authentic vintage 1950s American diner vibe and serves up everything you'd expect from hot dogs to milkshakes. You'll even find an authentic jukebox here too. It's just a few minutes from The Royal Mile, so fantastically located in the centre of Edinburgh and dogs are warmly welcomed.

DRUMMOHR CAMPING AND GLAMPING
Drummohr House Road, Musselburgh, EH21 8JS

Located just outside of Edinburgh, Dummohr is a great option if you want to relax in the countryside while being just close enough to Edinburgh city centre. There are a range of accommodation options, but I love the holiday lodges that come with a hot tub, and are peaceful and sheltered away from the hustle and bustle.

THE BALMORAL
1 Princes Street, EH2 2EQ

If you're looking for luxury The Balmoral ticks all the boxes. It's located in the grand clocktower in the heart of Edinburgh and just next to Waverley Station. Dogs receive their very own canine welcome package with a bed, bowl, treats, a bottle of Pawsecco and even a special bandana.

MOTEL ONE EDINBURGH-ROYAL
18 Market Street, EH1 1BL

Motel One sits proud in a listed sixteenth-century building in the middle of Edinburgh Old Town. You'll be perfectly located with The Royal Mile, Edinburgh Castle and more right on your doorstep. It's stylish and contemporary, and the rooms are a really affordable price point for the city. They welcome dogs, just let them know you'll be bringing your furry friend when you book.

20.

Isle of Arran

A gem of an island located just off the west coast of Scotland, the Isle of Arran is home to some beautiful landscapes and diverse terrain with an abundance of forests, coastal paths and mountains to explore.

It's often referred to as 'Scotland in Miniature' because it has every type of landscape associated with Scotland and the Big 5 – iconic British wildlife like golden eagles, seals, red deer, otters and red squirrels.

The best way to get here is by ferry, which takes just under an hour. The service is frequent, with several sailings daily.

Arran is renowned for its varied landscapes, including rugged highlands, gentle lowlands and coastal areas. One of the most popular dog-friendly spots is the Glenashdale Falls (known locally as Eas a' Chrannaig), located near the village of Whiting Bay. The trail is relatively easy and boasts fantastic views along the way, while dogs will love the chance to splash in the streams. It's a particularly stunning natural spectacle with a series of dramatic waterfalls tumbling gracefully down rocky steps.

For those who love coastal paths the Arran Coastal Way is a must-do. The 65-mile trail circles the entire island, with absolutely breathtaking views of the sea and coastline. The route passes through charming villages like Lamlash and Brodick, which are also well worth a visit and are fantastic places to stop and refresh.

Brodick itself is the island's main hub and where you'll find the legendary Brodick Castle. Perched majestically on the coast, the gardens and country park are dog friendly and provide commanding views of the surrounding landscape. The castle dates back to the thirteenth century, and as you wander the medieval grounds there is an air of mystery about the place. There is also a red squirrel hide in the grounds so keep your eyes peeled for a sighting!

The southern coast is also home to some gorgeous walking routes, including my favourite around the village of Blackwaterfoot. The scenic path meanders along the shore, offering delightful views of the sea. It's a gentle route and quite flat, making it a great option for a less strenuous walk.

Before you head off, be sure to stock up on goodies from the renowned Blackwaterfoot Bakery. You'll find the shelves stocked with amazing croissants, pastries, mouthwatering focaccias and sourdoughs. They operate an honesty box out of opening hours, but it's best to get there early to get the widest selection.

If you're after something a little more adventurous, try climbing Goatfell, the island's highest peak standing majestically at 874 metres above sea level. The hike to the summit is a rewarding challenge with rugged ridges and is definitely a more demanding route suited to well-versed hikers.

All this natural beauty is perfectly complemented by Arran's warm and welcoming local community, with many of the cafés and pubs being dog friendly.

Places to explore

GLENASHDALE FALLS
Glenashdale Forest, KA27 8QX

Located in the Isle of Arran's lush Glenashdale Forest, this series of beautiful waterfalls is fed by the glacial melt of the surrounding hills. The waterfalls are surrounded by woodlands and moss-covered boulders with several walking routes, making it the perfect tranquil and magical escape into nature.

BRODICK CASTLE, GARDEN AND COUNTRY PARK
Brodick, KA27 8HY

Nestled on the coast, Brodick Castle grounds and gardens are dog friendly and a treat for the senses with blooming rhododendrons, towering conifers, and serene paths that wind through the majestic and historic estate. You'll also get fantastic views over the island here, particularly to Goatfell, Arran's highest peak.

GOATFELL

Standing at 874 metres above sea level, this magnificent mountain has panoramic views of the island and beyond. It's a tricky walk and suited to those who are used to adventure, as the summit opens up to windswept, craggy heights. The weather can be unpredictable and change quickly here, so make sure to check the forecast before heading out and take appropriate clothing for you and your dog.

Places to eat, drink and stay 🐾🐾

LITTLE ROCK CAFÉ AND WEE DELI
Main Street, Brodick, KA27 8AJ

A gorgeous little shore front café with its very own dog-friendly section. You'll find sweeping views along the bay from here with a clean and contemporary feel inside, and great value food and drink. There's even a great deli too, where you can pick up high-quality goods from across Arran, Scotland and beyond.

THE OLD PIER CAFÉ
A841, Lamlash, KA27 8JN

This very dog-friendly café welcomes humans and their furry friends alike, serving a range of tasty baked goods, teas, coffees and lunches. It's a quaint and traditional place with wooden mish-mash tables and chalk board specials – perfect for warming up after exploring the local beauty.

AUCHRANNIE RESORT
Auchrannie Road, Brodick, KA27 8BZ

Perfect for pampered pooches, Auchrannie provides in-room treats and even fluffy towels for mucky paws after a day exploring the surrounding landscape. They have a range of rooms, but the retreats located in the grounds are particularly stunning, with floor-to-ceiling windows overlooking the rolling countryside.

THE CORRIE HOTEL
Shore Road, Corrie, KA27 8JB

Serving up fantastic Scottish fayre, The Corrie Hotel is a lovely spot to unwind after a long walk on the hills. There is an abundance of gorgeous mountain scenery right on the doorstep, so if it's sunny make sure you head out to the beer garden to soak it all in. Dog-friendly rooms are also available here if you're looking for somewhere to stay.

THE DOUGLAS HOTEL
Shore Road, Brodick, KA27 8AW

An ideal base on the island, The Douglas Hotel is just a stone's throw from the ferry terminal at Brodick, so you won't have to travel far once you arrive on the island. The hotel has a friendly feel about it with gorgeous views over Brodick Bay and Goatfell. Dogs are also welcome here and will soon sniff out the treat jar at reception.

WEE HOUSE
19A Hamilton Terrace, Lamlash, KA27 8LR

Only a few metres from the gorgeous Lamlash Beach, Wee House is a cosy cottage reminiscent of those on the Norwegian coast with beautiful blue wooden panelling. It's small, but well designed with open-plan living and sleeping up to four. And, of course, dog friendly too!

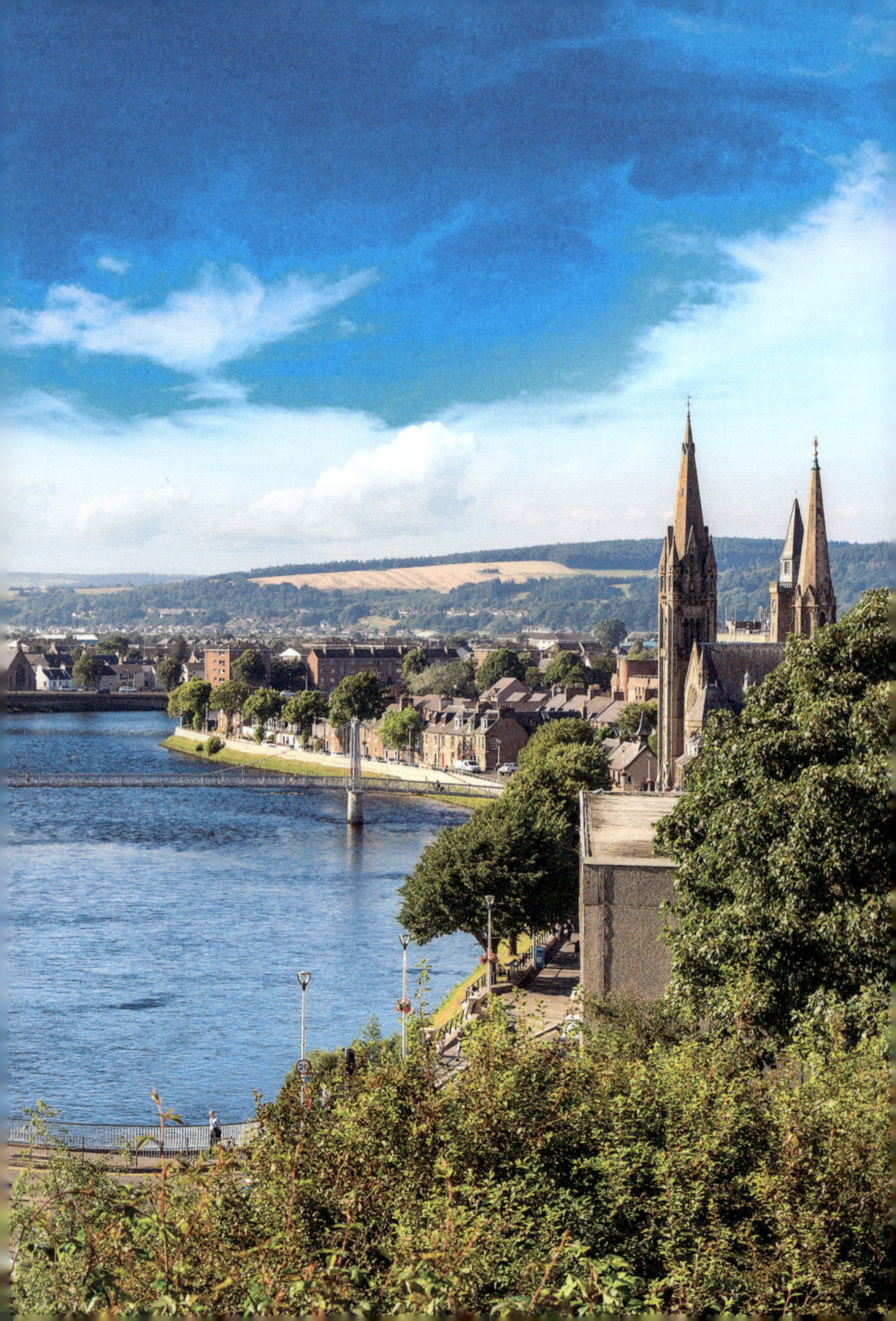

21.

Inverness

Known as the capital of the Scottish Highlands, Inverness is often the starting point of those looking to take on the NC500 road trip or explore the Highlands. Plus, there are a wealth of scenic walks in the area (some more challenging than others).

From the city centre itself, you can walk along the River Ness to the picturesque Ness Islands, a collection of wooded islets connected by charming Victorian footbridges. These peaceful islands are an excellent spot for a relaxing and steady walk, with plenty of benches en route to sit and enjoy the tranquil surroundings while your dog explores.

For those looking to be more adventurous, Inverness serves as the gateway to the iconic North Coast 500 (NC500), a 516-mile route around the northern coast of Scotland. This epic road trip, often referred to as Scotland's answer to Route 66, starts and ends in Inverness, making it an ideal base for your journey.

As you leave Inverness and head north, a popular first stop is the Black Isle, a peninsula famous for its traditional villages, rolling countryside and coastal views. One of the highlights here is Chanonry Point, considered one of the best places in the UK to spot bottlenose dolphins. The pebble beach is a great place for a walk with your dog while you keep an eye out to sea to try and spot some of the playful creatures in Moray Firth.

The route takes you through some of Scotland's most breathtaking landscapes, from desolate sandy beaches to towering mountains and serene lochs. It's dotted with dog-friendly stops, including several of the most stunning beaches, which look like they belong in the Caribbean. Two on my must-see list are Balnakeil Beach and

Achmelvich Bay, both of which boast white sand and clear blue waters, and best of all are dog friendly year-round.

Of course, a trip to the Highlands would also not be complete without a visit to the famous Loch Ness to see if you can catch a glimpse of Nessie, just 30 minutes outside of Inverness centre. Known worldwide for its mysterious monster, the area is also a walking haven surrounded by dense forests that frame the water's edge with a variety of hiking paths. Or if cruising is more your thing, jump aboard one of the many dog-friendly boat trips that are available in the area.

Places to explore

NC500

A bucket-list worthy road trip that starts in Inverness and loops around the northernmost reaches of Scotland, taking in an awe-inspiring mix of rugged coastlines, towering mountains and sweeping beaches. Perfect for dog-friendly adventures, the best way to do this route is hiring a campervan and braving the elements. I promise it will be an adventure you'll never forget.

CHANONRY POINT

Ness Road, Fortrose, IV10 8SD

Known as one of the best places in the UK to spot Dolphins, Chanonry Point is an unforgettable place to visit with sweeping views of the Moray Firth. You'll be able to walk along the pebble beach and grassy headland as your dog can explore the wide, open spaces here and natural beauty of the place. Make sure to head up to the iconic lighthouse here too for some fantastic photo opportunities.

LOCH NESS

Located just a short drive from Inverness, this iconic destination is steeped in history and surrounded by amazing scenery. The vast deep waters of the loch stretch for 23 miles, with numerous walking trails along its shores where dogs can enjoy the fresh Highland air as you traverse through forest paths, open hillsides and alongside the famous loch. You might even catch a glimpse of the legendary Loch Ness Monster!

Places to eat, drink and stay

CASTLE TAVERN
1 View Place, IV2 4SA

Situated with direct and unspoilt views of Inverness Castle and just steps from the River Ness, Castle Tavern is a charming dog-friendly pub offering the perfect spot to unwind. On a sunny day enjoy the outdoor seating where you can take in the picturesque castle and river views. Dogs are welcome inside and out.

BLACK ISLE BAR
68 Church Street, IV1 1EN

Located in the heart of Inverness city centre, Black Isle Bar is a vibrant, dog-friendly brewery that specialises in craft beers and wood-fired pizzas, a winning combination. There's a laid-back atmosphere here with dogs welcome throughout. Don't forget to check out the secret rooftop garden too.

KINGSMILL HOTEL
Culcabock Road, IV2 3LP

For a luxurious dog-friendly stay in Inverness, Kingsmill Hotel has elegant rooms and spacious grounds. Its proximity to the city's sights makes it an ideal base for exploring the city and beyond. The dog-friendly rooms here are all on the ground floor, making it easy to access the hotel's gorgeous gardens.

DORES INN
B862, Dores, IV2 6TR

Nestled at the southern tip of Loch Ness, Dores Inn has impressive views of the famous loch from its expansive beer garden – views don't get much better than this! The pub is known for its warm and welcoming atmosphere, where both humans and dogs are treated with Highland hospitality. The perfect spot to unwind after a day of adventure.

LOCH NESS INN
Lewiston, Drumnadrochit, IV63 6UW

Situated in the Highland village of Drumnadrochit, Loch Ness Inn is perfectly located for exploring the famous loch, with a range of walking trails right on the doorstep. Inspired by the lochs and glens of the Highlands, the bedrooms here are all individually designed and boast a contemporary and luxury feel.

PINEWOOD STEADING
Easter Street, South Clunes, IV5 7PT

If you're looking to be submersed in nature this peaceful and secluded lodge is perfect, located in 3.5 acres of birch woods and pine trees with captivating and uninterrupted views. You'll find some of the most spectacular scenery and mountain ranges in all of Scotland on your doorstep, but you can also enjoy amazing views right from the lodge windows, which look out over the Beauly Firth and the Black Isle.

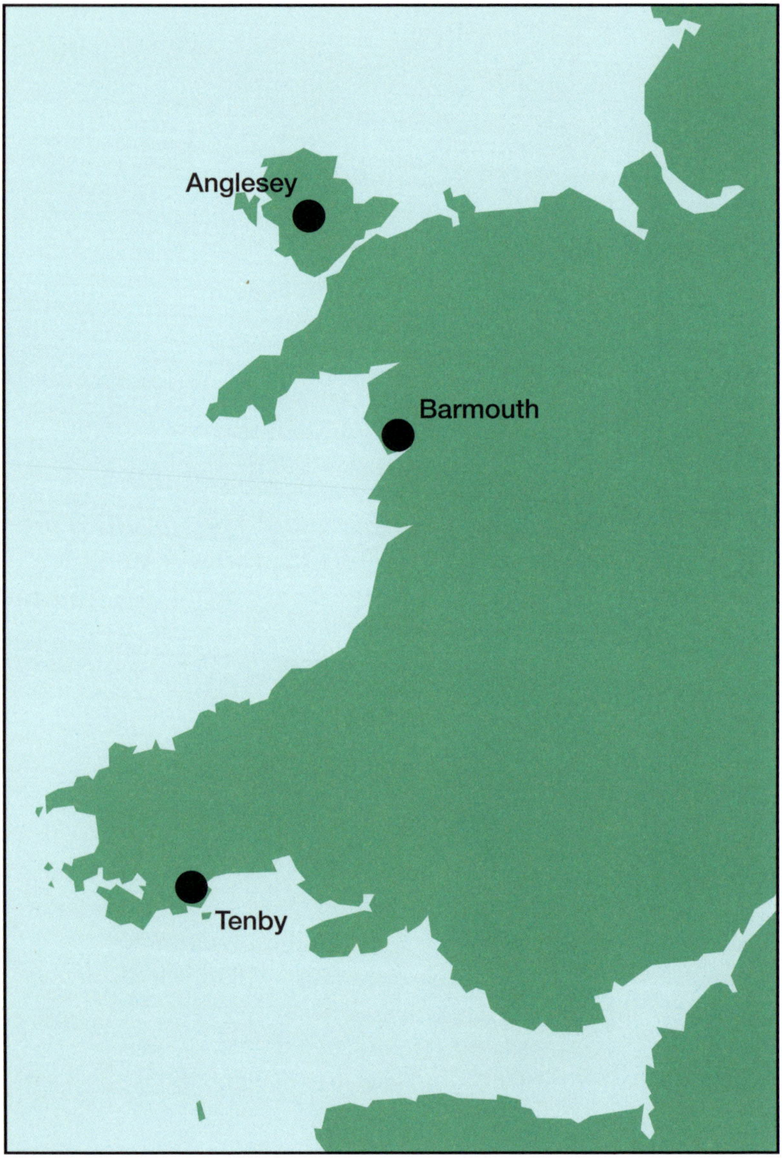
Anglesey
Barmouth
Tenby

Wales

Barmouth   165

Tenby   171

Anglesey   179

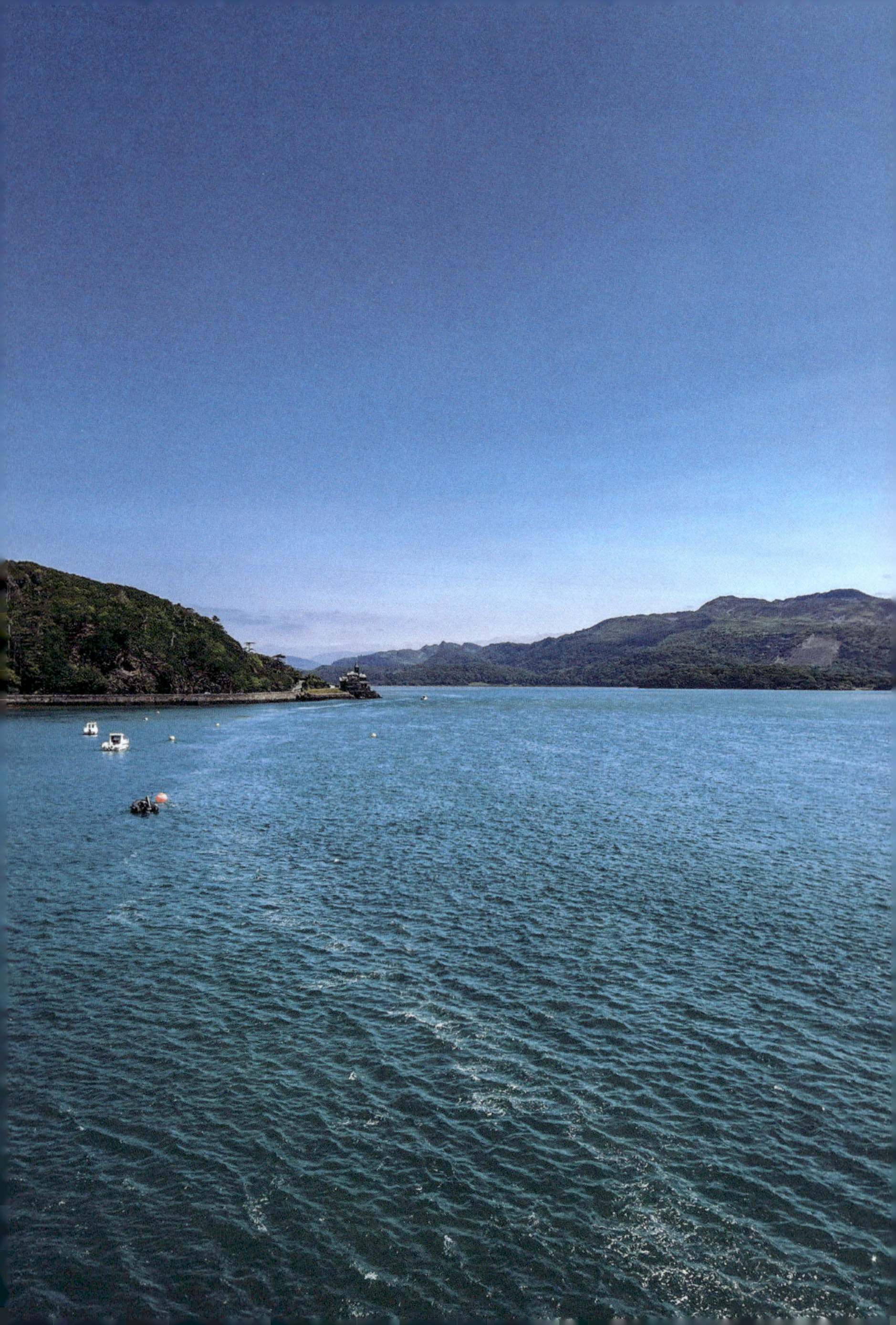

22.

Barmouth

Located on the southern coast of Snowdonia in Wales, Barmouth (Abermaw) is perfectly nestled between the majestic mountains and the expansive Cardigan Bay.

The centrepiece of Barmouth is its beautiful sandy beach, Traeth Abermaw, which has a dog-friendly section year-round and stretches for miles.

There are also a range of scenic and coastal walks you can take right from the centre of town. The Mawddach Trail follows a former railway line running alongside the estuary, offering a flat, easy walking terrain. The route is 9 miles long, so doable in a day if you are up for the challenge with plenty of open spaces and shaded woodland along the route.

If you don't fancy walking quite as far, I recommend the slightly shorter walk down to Penrhyn Point, where you can catch the pedestrian ferry back to Barmouth Harbour with your dog by your side. It's also a great way to see more of the town's picturesque waterfront from an alternative viewpoint.

The Panorama Walk is another fantastic route, which takes you above Barmouth and, as it implies in the name, offers panoramic vistas of the town, estuary and the distant peaks of Eryri (Snowdon). The trail can be steep in places, but it's well worth the effort, and there are several benches along the way where you can rest and take in the views.

Of course, Barmouth is also just a short distance to Eryri National Park (Snowdonia) where there are walks in abundance. Only about 20 minutes away by car, Eryri offers an array of outdoor adventures with diverse landscapes including forests, lakes and mountains, with numerous trails to pick from.

If you're looking for nature you won't be disappointed here, with ample opportunities to spot a variety of species in their natural habitat. The Mawddach Valley RSPB Arthog Bog is a haven for bird watchers, and dogs are welcome on the trails on a lead. It's a small wetland reserve but is crammed full of wildlife including flocks of siskins and long-tailed tits alongside rare flowers, butterflies and even grass snakes.

Beyond the natural beauty, Barmouth is also exceptionally welcoming to dogs, and you'll often find water bowls outside the local shops and restaurants as you stroll along the promenade.

Places to explore

ERYRI NATIONAL PARK (SNOWDONIA)

Eryri National Park, known formerly as Snowdonia, is right on the doorstep of Barmouth and well worth a visit while in the area. It has some of the most dramatic landscapes in Wales, with towering peaks, rolling valleys and shimmering lakes, and is a haven for adventurous walkers and their canine companions. You'll be able to climb Snowdon (Yr Wyddfa) here, the highest mountain in Wales, as well as take on less challenging trails that wind through ancient woodlands and open moorlands.

FAIRBOURNE RAILWAY

Beach Road, Fairbourne, LL38 2EX

Just across the estuary from Barmouth, this charming narrow-gauge railway runs along the beautiful Mawddach Estuary, surrounded by sweeping views of mountains, marshes and sandy dunes. Dogs are welcome to ride the train with you, making it a fun and relaxing way to take in the coastal scenery. At the end of the line, Fairbourne Beach is the perfect place for a seaside stroll with your dog, where peaceful views over the water to Barmouth in the distance make for a memorable day out.

PANORAMA WALK

Panorama Walk, LL42 1DX

Accessible right from Barmouth itself, Panorama Walk is a stunning dog-friendly walking trail with (as the name suggests) panoramic views over the Mawddach Estuary and Cardigan Bay. The 4-mile route winds through varied woodland and country roads, opening up to beautiful vistas stretching out to the sea, estuary and peaks of Eryri National Park.

Places to eat, drink and stay 🐾🐾

THE DAVY JONES LOCKER
The Quay, LL42 1ET

Located down on The Quay, The Davy Jones Locker is a fantastic dog-friendly café that is perfectly positioned right on the beachfront. It's an ideal spot for brunch or lunch while soaking in the coastal views. The staff are all super friendly here, and there is a high chance your dog will receive copious amounts of fuss!

GOODIES COFFEE SHOP
33 High Street, LL42 1DW

This quirky café combines a relaxed, eclectic vibe with a warm, welcoming atmosphere for both you and your canine companion. Inside you'll be greeted by an inviting blend of vintage furnishings and unique décor, where you can cosy up and enjoy a coffee and cake while your dog lounges comfortably at your side.

BAE ABERMAW HOTEL
Panorama Road, LL42 1DQ

With spectacular coastal views, Bae Abermaw Hotel is located just a short walk from the town's picturesque beach. The hotel has a range of stylish and comfortable rooms, which provide a relaxing haven after a day of exploration, and friendly staff will make sure your dog feels right at home.

BARMOUTH BAY AWAY RESORTS

Holiday Village, Barmouth Bay Holiday Park,
Tal-y-bont, LL43 2BJ

A perfect family friendly option, the resort offers a wide range of dog-friendly accommodation including spacious lodges that are perfect for unwinding in after a day exploring the area. It also boasts direct beach access alongside other amenities, such as an indoor heated pool, sports courts and even hot tubs.

SHOWMAN'S WAGON

Taicynhaeaf, Dolgellau, LL40 2TU

Is there anything cooler than saying you've stayed in a 1950s fairground caravan?! This lovingly renovated wagon is nestled in the scenic Mawddach Estuary near Dolgellau and offers a charming dog-friendly retreat with a difference. It perfectly combines vintage allure with modern comfort, creating a cosy haven amid the stunning landscapes of Eryri National Park.

THE LAST INN

Church Street, LL42 1EL

A charming fifteenth-century gem, The Last Inn is renowned as one of Wales's most iconic inns. It's nestled close to the heart of Barmouth and offers a warm and friendly atmosphere. Inside, the inn is brimming with history and tales, adorned with wooden beams salvaged from old ships and nautical décor that evokes the rich maritime history of the area.

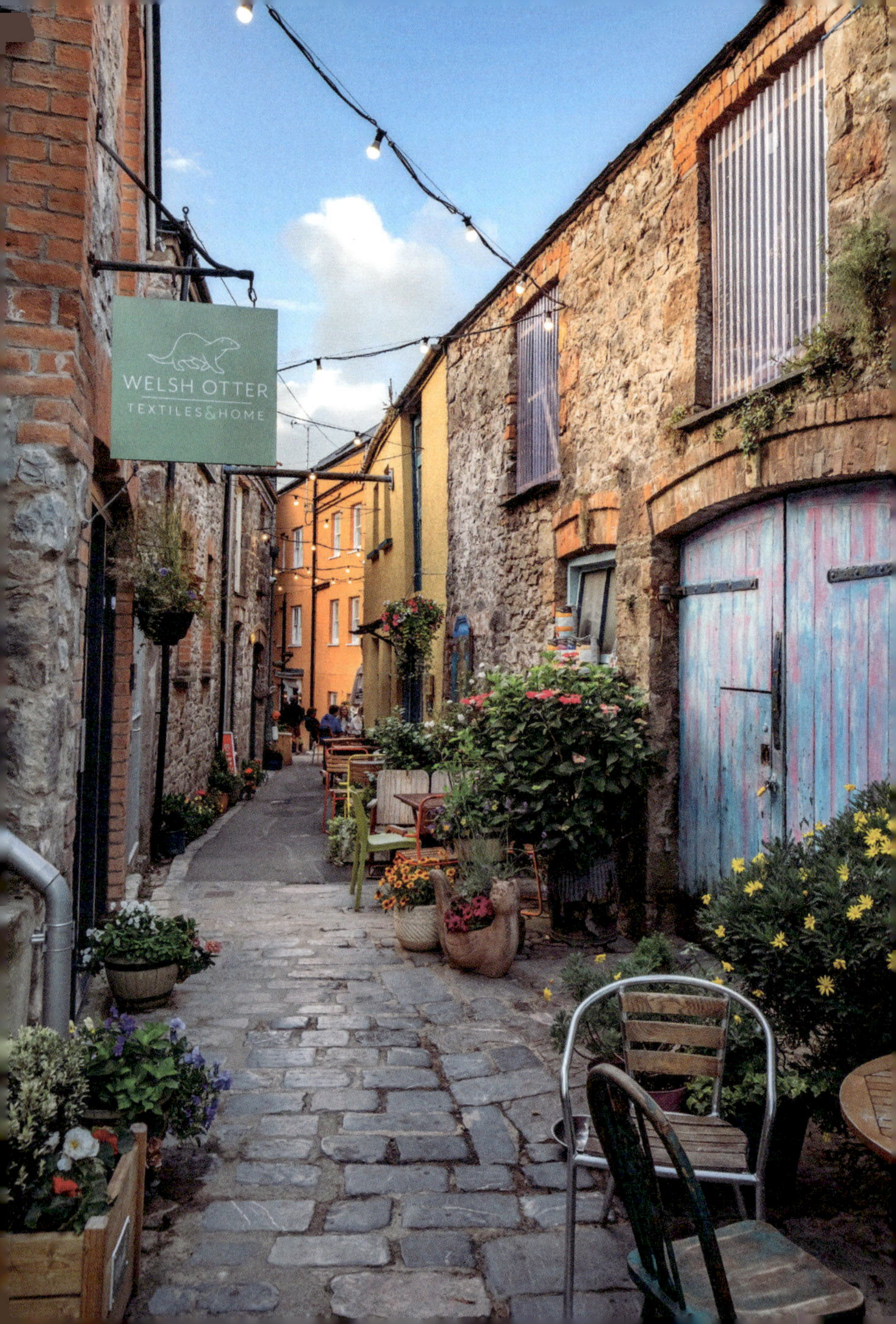
WELSH OTTER
TEXTILES&HOME

23.

Tenby

With its exquisite coastal scenery, historic buildings and welcoming atmosphere, Tenby (Dinbych-y-Pysgod) is teeming with dog-friendly things to do – from exploring the town's cobbled streets, to enjoying the beautiful beaches.

Known for its picture perfect and vibrant harbour, Tenby is one of the top seaside towns in Wales, and there is nothing better than watching the boats come and go at dusk while you tuck into fresh fish and chips with your dog by your side.

A highlight of any visit to Tenby is a boat trip to Caldey Island. Just a short journey across the water, this serene island is a haven of tranquillity and natural beauty. Owned and run by a community of Cistercian monks, it's open to the public on summer weekdays and Saturdays. Dogs are welcome on many of the boat rides, making it easy to make sure they're not left out. Once on the island you can explore its scenic trails, visit the enchanting village and enjoy the peaceful surroundings.

Back on the mainland there is an abundance of scenic walks, and the Pembrokeshire Coast Path offers some of the most breathtaking views in the region. The long-distance trail runs along the length of the coastline, and the section near Tenby towards Saundersfoot is particularly stunning.

If you don't mind travelling a little further afield, consider a visit to the nearby Gower Peninsula, a designated Area of Outstanding Natural Beauty. The peninsula boasts a rich tapestry of coastal heathlands and rocky cliffs, serving as the perfect backdrop to the many walks and trails you can take from here. Rhossili Bay is

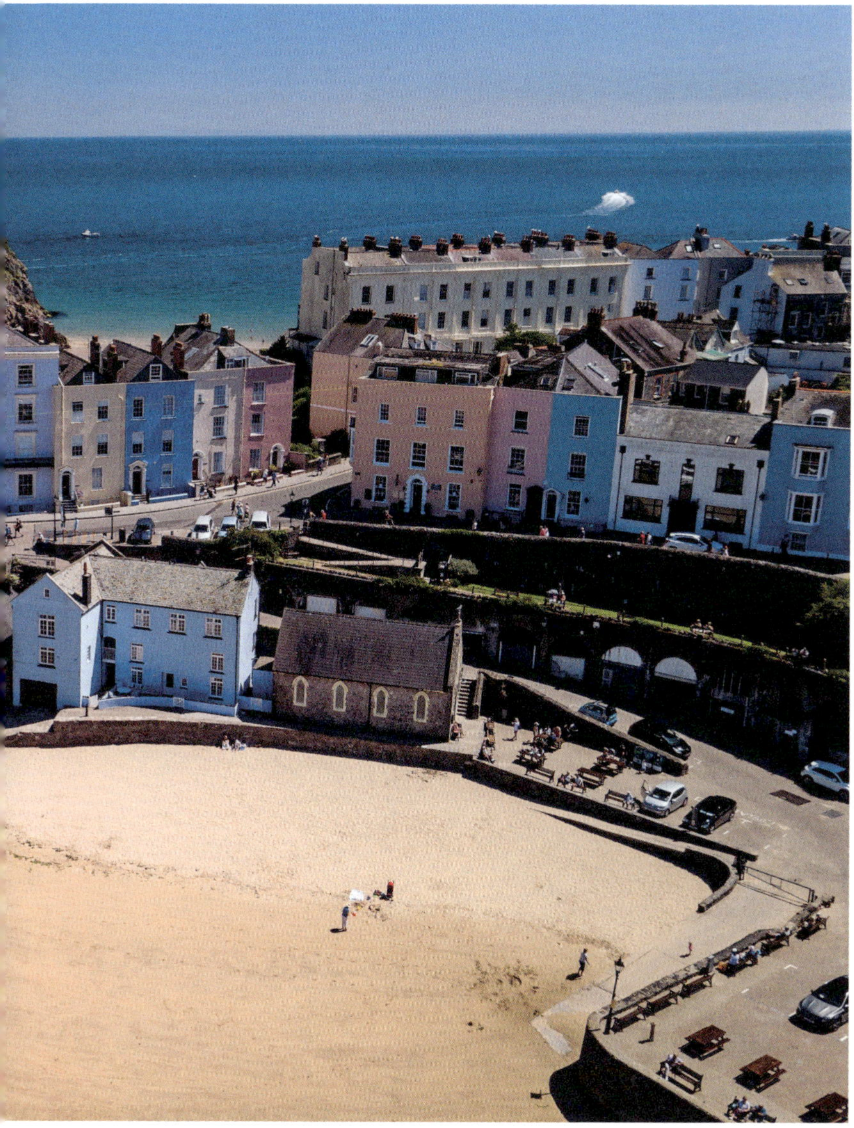

particularly beautiful, alongside Worm's Head, a dramatic headland with a unique shape.

Another spot not to be missed is Carew Castle, a fantastic historical site that welcomes dogs on leads. This medieval fortress, with imposing walls and scenic moat, offers a fascinating glimpse into Wales's past. The castle's expansive grounds provide plenty of space for a leisurely walk, making it a great place to visit for history buffs and dog owners alike.

And like any perfect seaside destination, Tenby has its own dog-friendly beach. South Beach is a huge expanse of golden sand stretching out over a mile, with unrestricted access for dogs throughout the year.

Places to explore

CALDEY ISLAND
Ferry Kiosk, Penniless Cove Hill, SA70 7BZ

Nestled off the coast of Pembrokeshire, Caldey Island is accessible by a short boat ride from Tenby and is a serene island that offers a picturesque escape with scenic trails, sandy beaches and stunning coastal views. Dogs are welcome on the island, where you can explore tranquil pathways along the rugged shoreline.

GOWER PENINSULA
Rhossili, Swansea, SA3 1PR

The first area in the UK to be designated as an Area of Outstanding Natural Beauty, Gower Peninsula is a treasure trove of dog-friendly walks. Dogs will enjoy the freedom of vast stretches of coastline, such as Rhossili Bay and Three Cliffs Bay, where they can run free and roam the expansive sands.

SOUTH BEACH
The Esplanade, SA70 7EG

Dog friendly year-round, South Beach stretches for miles and is perfect for long walks or just sitting and enjoying the peaceful sounds of the waves coming and going against the golden shores. The beach is also close to the town, meaning local amenities are never far away.

Places to eat, drink and stay 🐾🐾

FUCHSIA CAFÉ
Upper Frog St, SA70 7JD

Known for its friendly staff, gorgeous décor and delightful atmosphere, this café serves a range of tasty treats including a special dog menu. It's a great spot for unwinding after a day of exploring the beautiful Tenby coastline and for humans, the cookies are to die for!

HARBWR BREWERY TAP & KITCHEN
Julian's Street, SA70 7AS

Located in the heart of Tenby, Harbwr Brewery Tap & Kitchen is a great spot for a hearty meal or a quick drink. They serve fantastic roast dinners and locally brewed craft beers, making it a fantastic spot to wind down after a day of adventure.

SALTY'S BEACH BAR & RESTAURANT
Water's Edge, South Beach, SA70 7EG

Conveniently perched on the shores of Tenby's South Beach, Salty's has a delectable menu of mouthwatering fresh, local seafood. Dogs are welcome inside and out, but on a sunny day, make sure you enjoy the garden, where you and your dog can enjoy the sea breeze and gorgeous surroundings.

PENALLY ABBEY HOTEL
Penally, SA70 7PY

Penally Abbey couldn't be better located, just a 10-minute walk from the Pembrokeshire Coastal Path and wonderful Penally Beach. This elegant accommodation features four bedrooms that open directly on to beautifully maintained gardens, allowing easy access for you and your dog to explore the outside space. You can open your door and walk straight out onto the beach here, it really doesn't get much better than that!

ALADDIN SAFARI TENT
Redberth Gardens, SA70 8RP

If you're looking for something a little more unique, Aladdin Safari Tent provides a dog-friendly glamping experience within a short drive of Pembrokeshire Coast National Park and Tenby. It's spacious and comfortable, but the best part is the scenic views right from the garden.

THE ESPLANADE
1 Esplanade, SA70 7DU

The Esplanade is a gorgeous guest house with spectacular views over to Caldey Island. It's small with only 14 bedrooms, meaning you get a personal touch from the owners who are extremely welcoming and friendly. They're also super dog friendly here, and dogs are welcome at no extra charge.

24.

Anglesey

The largest island in Wales and the jewel of the northern coast, Anglesey (Ynys Môn) is famous for its spectacular landscapes across the nearly 125 miles of coastline that is a designated Area of Outstanding Natural Beauty (AONB). It's no wonder, as everywhere you look there are sand dunes, cliffs, pebble and pretty beaches, ensuring every walk is filled with new sights and scents for you and your dog to enjoy.

The area is a haven for wildlife, not least Puffin Island, which is uninhabited and located off the eastern tip of Anglesey and can actually be travelled to on a dog-friendly boat trip from Beaumaris.

True to its name it's one of the best places in Wales to see puffins alongside colonies of razorbills, guillemots and a variety of other seabirds. You might even spot a grey seal lounging on the rocks or bobbing in the surrounding waters.

You can't miss visiting South Stack Lighthouse, one of the most iconic landmarks in Wales, which is perched on a rocky islet. To reach the lighthouse you'll have to descend a steep 400-step staircase winding down the cliffside, however, you'll be rewarded with amazing views of the coastline and swirling sea below.

The coastal path itself is also not to be missed, spanning the entire perimeter of the island and stretching over 200 miles. One of my favourite sections runs from Moelfre to Red Wharf Bay. Approximately 6 miles, this section takes you along some of the most photogenic parts of the coastline, with sheltered coves and sandy beaches.

You'll start in the village of Moelfre with its whitewashed cottages and eventually come to Traeth Lligwy, a gorgeous beach, which is

usually quieter than some of the more popular spots, making it an ideal place to enjoy the natural beauty without the crowds.

Elsewhere, you'll also find an abundance of beautiful beaches that are dog friendly year-round including Porth Trecastell, also known as Cable Bay, and Aberffraw Beach to name but a few.

One of Anglesey's highlights is the picturesque village of Beaumaris, known for its medieval castle and vibrant waterfront. Here, you can stroll around the town's historic streets and along the pier, where you can watch the boats and even catch a glimpse of some local wildlife including seabirds and raptors.

Places to explore

BOAT TRIP TO PUFFIN ISLAND
Seacoast Safaris, Pier House, Beaumaris, LL58 8BS

Departing from the scenic coastal town of Beaumaris, take one of the many dog-friendly boat trips where you can cruise across the sparkling water leaving the rugged, dramatic coastline behind you as you sail around Puffin Island. During the summer breeding season, the island is teeming with puffins and other seabirds, and occasionally seals bask on the rocky shores too.

TRAETH LLIGWY BEACH
Lligwy Dulas, Moelfre, LL70 9PQ

A beautiful, sandy and most importantly dog-friendly year-round beach, Traeth Lligwy is a real gem on the Anglesey coast. The backdrop of rolling low sand dunes, adorned with hardy coastal grasses and wildflowers adds a touch of vibrant colour, while the sweeping views of the Irish Sea extend to the horizon – it really is a beautiful place to visit.

SOUTH STACK LIGHTHOUSE
Holyhead, LL65 1YH

Perched on a dramatic cliff on Anglesey's western coast, South Stack Lighthouse is a postcard perfect backdrop to some amazing walks. The iconic lighthouse, built in 1809, stands sentinel over treacherous waters and can be accessed via a steep staircase and scenic walk through rugged terrain.

Places to eat, drink and stay

THE WHITE EAGLE
Rhoscolyn, Holyhead, LL65 2NJ

The décor in here is contemporary and bright and the beer garden has gorgeous views stretching out over the coastline and countryside. You can expect some delicious seafood among other seasonal specials. Dogs are welcomed here, receiving a water bowl and treats on arrival!

OYSTER CATCHER
Maelog Lake, Rhosneigr, LL64 5JP

Nestled in the centre of Rhosneigr, the Oyster Catcher serves up a menu of fresh, locally sourced seafood and traditional pub grub. Dogs are given a friendly reception, with their own water bowls, making it a great spot to enjoy a meal after a walk along the nearby beach.

STAG INN
High Street, Caemes, LL67 0EW

With traditional décor and a hearty menu, this village pub is welcoming and quaint, and an ideal spot to unwind with your dog by your side. The staff are welcoming and well accustomed to furry visitors, making sure they give them plenty of fuss and treats too.

TÝ-CHI COTTAGE
Caeau Brychion, Niwbwrch, Llanfairpwllgwyngyll, LL61 6TL

Located near the picturesque Llanddwyn Beach, Tŷ-Chi Cottage is a delightful choice for those looking to enjoy a peaceful dog-friendly retreat. The cottage is beautifully appointed and has easy access to nearby trails and beach walks. The perfect spot to relax and soak up the coastal scenery.

AFON MENAI
Brynsiencyn, LL61 6NX

A beautiful holiday cottage located near the stunning Menai Strait, Afon Menai is well equipped and the perfect base for exploring the natural beauty of Anglesey. It's ideally located near scenic walks and dog-friendly beaches, and even has a hot tub to relax in after a long day exploring.

LASTRA FARM HOTEL
Penrhyd, Amlwch, LL68 9TF

Set in a luxurious and lovingly restored farmhouse, Lastra Farm is located in the north of the island surrounded by lush rolling fields at every turn. Dogs are treated like royalty here too and, gifted a goody bag on arrival with a new toy, bag of treats, and if they're lucky, a sausage at breakfast too. Plus, there are an abundance of walks straight from the door, and staff are always on hand to offer knowledgeable advice.

Battersea

Brighton

Isle of Wight

South East

Battersea	187
Brighton	193
Isle of Wight	201

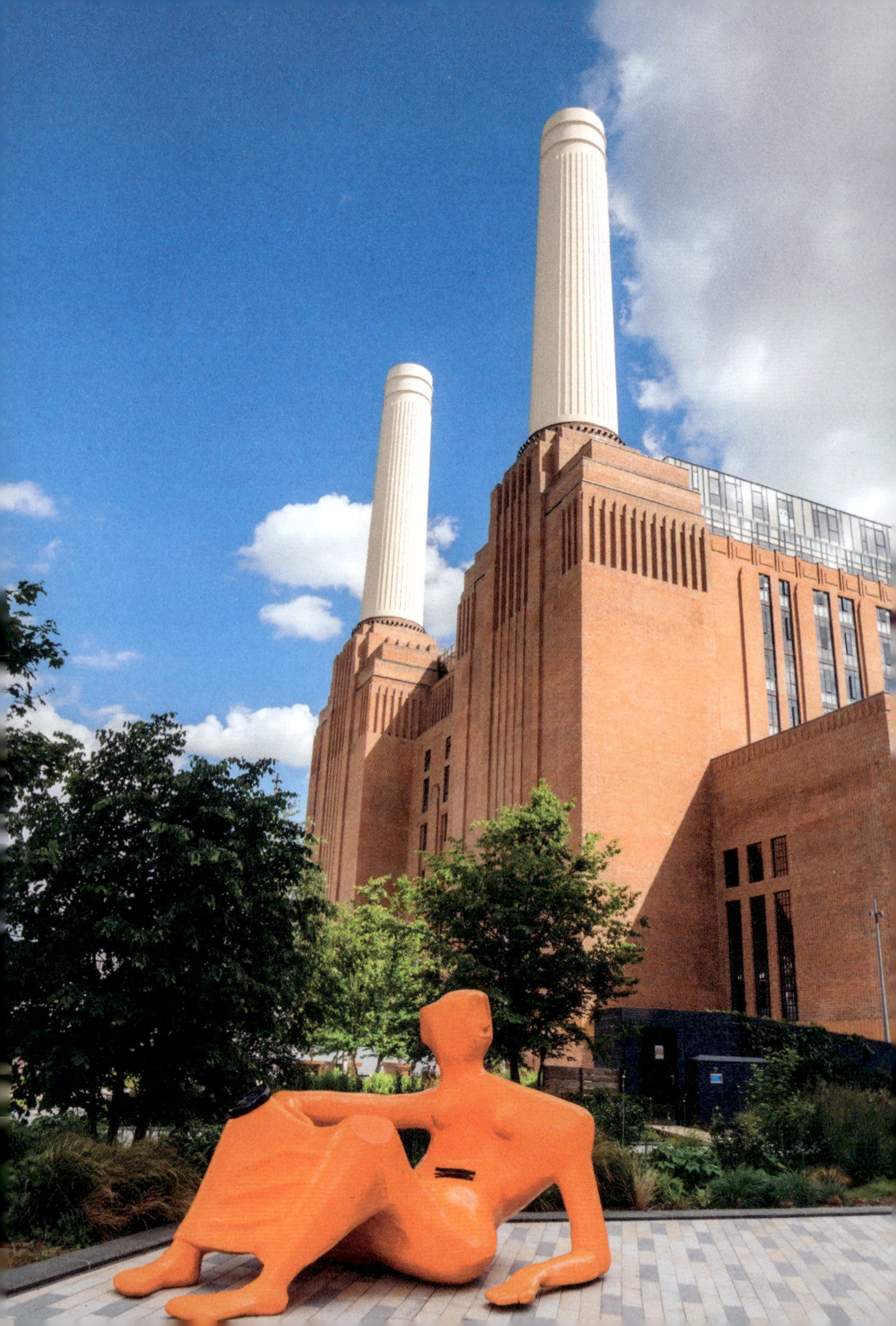

25.

Battersea

London might not be the first place you think of when considering a dog-friendly stay, but it's definitely a dark horse and quickly becoming one of my top destinations. It might be busy, but there are loads of dog-friendly things to do and some amazing green spaces to boot.

Battersea, nestled on the south bank of the Thames, is a fantastic place to base yourself when visiting the capital, and has quickly become popular among dog owners.

A notable landmark in the area is the recently reopened Battersea Power Station, a Grade II* listed building, which has been redeveloped into a modern shopping and leisure destination. Many shops, bars and restaurants allow dogs to accompany their owners inside and some even go the extra mile offering water bowls and treats.

Walking in London should also not be underestimated. The Thames Path is a particularly favourite route of mine as it's flat and allows you to spot so many sights along the way, such as the London Eye, the Houses of Parliament, the Tower of London and even Shakespeare's Globe.

For a great day out, I'd recommend hopping on one of the Thames Clippers. There is a station at Battersea Power Station, jump on and enjoy the wind in your hair (and fur) as you travel down the river to Greenwich, a bustling part of London that feels like you've escaped the city.

No visit here is complete without a stroll around Greenwich Park, one of the largest and oldest Royal Parks in London. It covers 183 acres and offers vast open spaces and well-maintained paths,

combined with the perfect mix of stunning panoramic views over the city skyline, natural beauty and cultural heritage.

Make sure you head up the steep hill to the Royal Observatory where you'll be able to take in sweeping views over the River Thames from the futuristic skyline of Canary Wharf to the historic architecture of the Maritime Museum below.

You'll also find a hoard of dog-friendly restaurants, cafés and pubs here, perfect to round off the day's exploring.

Places to explore

BATTERSEA POWER STATION
Circus Road West, Nine Elms, SW11 8DD

Steeped in industrial history, the Grade II* Battersea Power Station is full of dog-friendly shops and restaurants and is not to be missed. It's a fantastic place to explore and has an expansive outdoor area too.

TOWER BRIDGE ENGINE ROOMS
Tower Bridge Road, SE1 2UP

Located within the historic Tower Bridge, explore the fascinating exhibits here and learn more about the history and engineering of the marvel of Tower Bridge, all while your dog accompanies you. Dogs are allowed throughout the museum and even over the glass floor walkway!

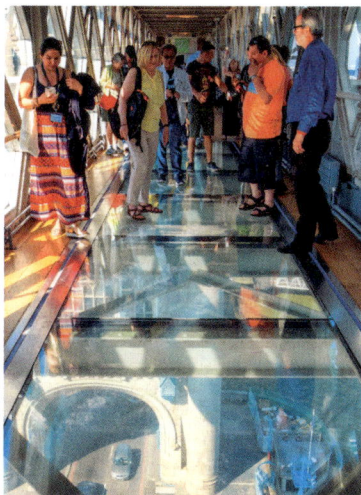

GREENWICH PARK
Greenwich, SE10 8QY

One of London's most cherished Royal Parks, and a fantastic place to escape the city with expansive green spaces. Spectacular views can be enjoyed away from the crowds while your dog runs and explores at the summit of One Tree Hill, which has long been a magnet for artists and writers.

Places to eat, drink and stay 🐾🐾

BREAD STREET KITCHEN & BAR
1st Floor, Battersea Power Station, Nine Elms,
SW11 8DD

One of Gordon Ramsay's restaurants, you can expect to find amazing tasting food in an upmarket setting. Dogs are welcomed in the bar here, so you can enjoy the stylish interior and relaxed vibe while you enjoy their modern take on British classics together.

GLORIA
54-56 Great Eastern Street, EC2A 3QR

Fun and eclectic are the first words that come to mind when trying to describe Gloria. It has a playful 1970s Capri aesthetic, transporting you to the Amalfi Coast with lush greenery and colourful décor. Known for its inviting atmosphere it embraces dogs with open arms too.

ROYAL LANCASTER
Lancaster Terrace, W2 2TY

A dog-sitting service, breathtaking views, even afternoon tea for dogs, Royal Lancaster is up there when it comes to the best luxury dog-friendly stays. Located just opposite Hyde Park and just a short walk from Paddington Station, it's a fantastic location for exploring the city.

BOROUGH MARKET

8 Southwark Street, SE1 1TL

One of London's oldest and most renowned food markets, Borough Market isn't just a place to grab an amazing bite to eat, but an experience too. Hidden between the railway lines of London Bridge, this vibrant market is a sensory delight of sights, sounds and smells, and has a diverse array of food and drink options. Plus, the market is dog friendly, so you can explore all of this without leaving your dog out.

NATIVE BANKSIDE

Empire Warehouse, 1 Bear Gardens, SE1 9ED

A historic warehouse packed with personality, Native Bankside is an aparthotel, so perfect if you want a little more space. They have a genuinely dog-friendly approach and provide water bowls and treats, with staff going above and beyond to make sure your dog feels as comfortable as you do. Plus, it's in a prime location just steps away from Borough Market and riverside walks along the Thames.

THE ALMA

499 Old York Road, SW18 1TF

Housed in an iconic landmark in Wandsworth Town, The Alma is a traditional Victorian pub and hotel. This hotel exudes a warm and inviting timeless appeal with each room thoughtfully designed. Dogs can expect to be treated to their very own hamper on arrival, so they'll feel right at home straight away.

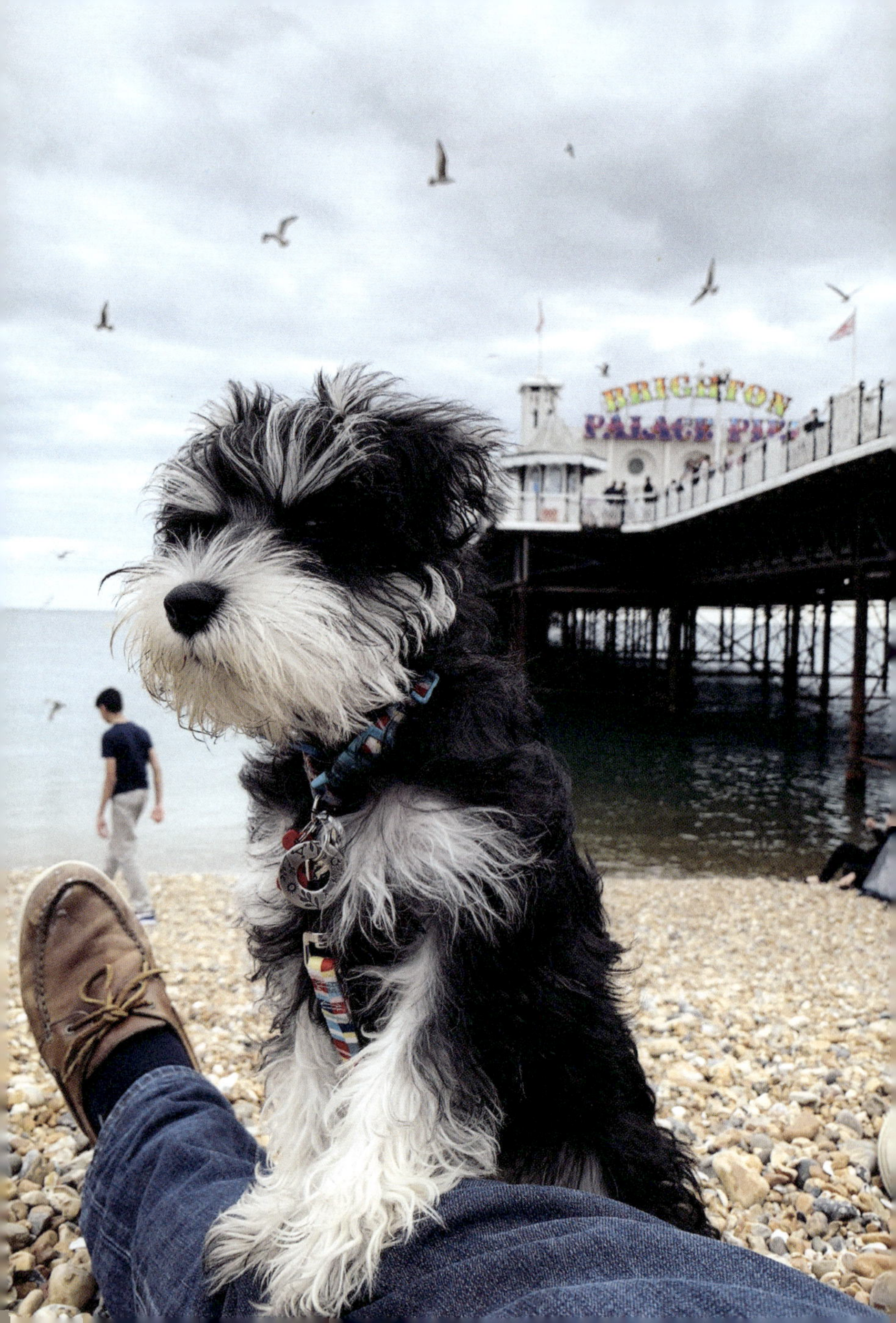
BRIGHTON
PALACE PI

26.

Brighton

A vibrant seaside town, Brighton has a bohemian vibe, beautiful coastline and an amazing array of dog-friendly things to do, places to walk and places to visit.

One of the main attractions is the expansive pebbly beach that stretches for miles along the coast, with dog-friendly sections year-round making it the perfect spot for a seaside frolic. After a long walk on the beach, you'll find plenty of dog-friendly beachside cafés where you can enjoy a coffee or ice cream, while taking in the salty sea breeze.

An iconic landmark in Brighton, The Royal Pavilion makes the perfect backdrop to any photo with your dog. The Royal Pavilion Gardens are dog friendly and a delight to walk through with exotic architecture, well-maintained paths and plenty of places to enjoy a rest including deckchairs!

Another must-visit area is The Lanes, a maze of narrow, winding streets filled with an eclectic mix of boutiques, cafés and antique shops. The district is a great area to explore with your dog as you discover hidden gems with many being dog friendly.

Of course, Brighton is not just a seaside city, but also a fantastic starting point for a variety of amazing walks exploring the beautiful landscapes of the South Coast and South Downs National Park.

The South Downs Way stretches over 100 miles across the South Downs National Park, and several sections are easily accessible from Brighton. Devil's Dyke, a legendary beauty spot, is one you can't miss.

This stunning V-shaped valley is surrounded by spectacular countryside, and you can walk from the outskirts of Brighton. There's a dog-friendly pub, which in my book scores top marks for a dog-friendly walk! You can retrace your steps back or if you're ready to give your feet a rest, there is a bus back to the city.

Places to explore

ROYAL PAVILION GARDENS

North Street, New Road, BN1 1FN

Wrapping round the iconic Royal Pavilion, the gardens that surround it offer a unique blend of regency grandeur and natural beauty. There are a variety of winding pathways to explore for both you and your dog, where you can admire the vibrant flower beds, exotic plants and sweeping lawns, all set against the backdrop of the Pavilion's striking and eclectic architecture.

VOLKS ELECTRIC RAILWAY

285 Madeira Drive, BN2 1EN

The oldest operating electric railway in the world, this charming train runs along the coast from the Palace Pier to Black Rock and is a delightful way to explore the seafront with your dog by your side, in fact, dogs even travel for free. The carriages are all historic with original wooden seats, and transport you back in time as you enjoy the refreshing sea breeze.

DEVIL'S DYKE

Devil's Dyke Road, BN1 8YJ

A magnificent natural gem, Devil's Dyke is a vast V-shaped valley carved out by natural forces over thousands of years and is only a short drive or bus journey away from Brighton city centre. The area has well-marked walking routes, which pass through fields dotted with wildflowers in the summer, while birds of prey such as kestrels or red kites can often be seen soaring overhead.

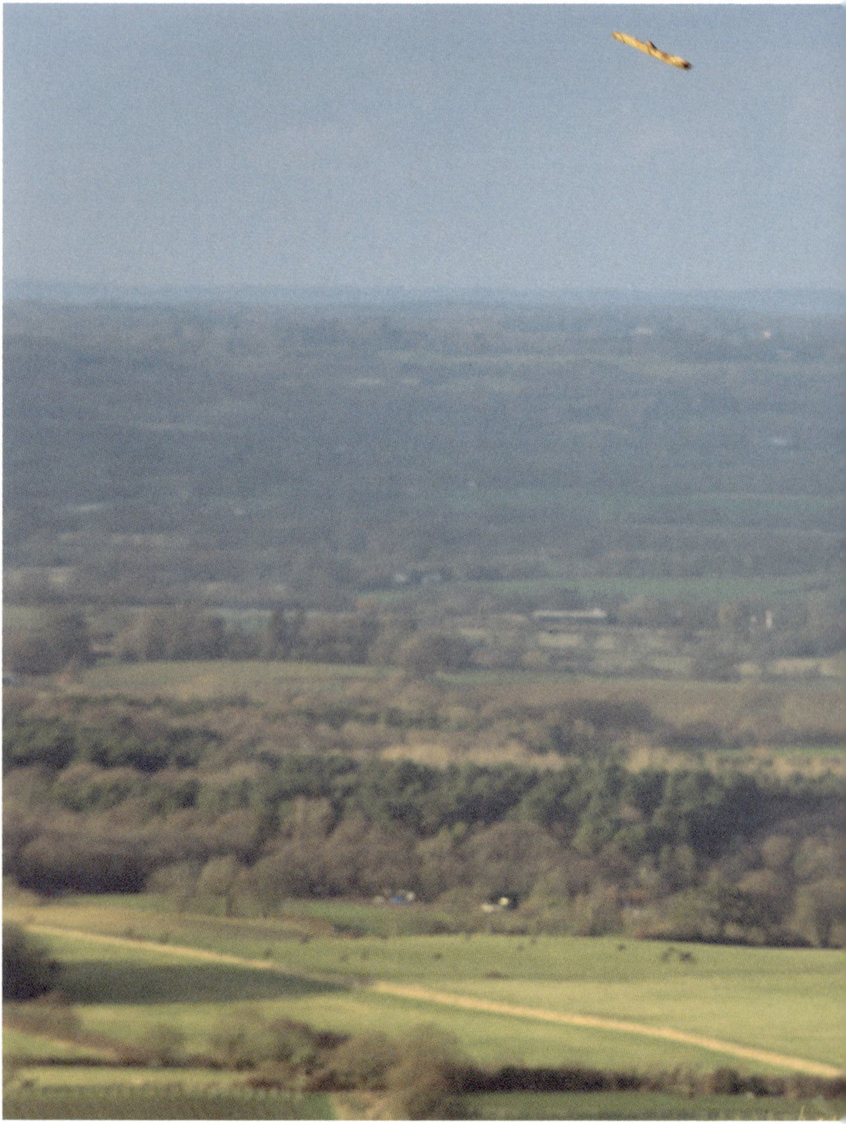

Places to eat, drink and stay 🐾🐾

COPPA CLUB
12–16 Brighton Square, BN1 1HD

Tucked away down a labyrinth of narrow streets you'll stumble across Coppa Club, a cosy and intimate bar and restaurant where you can enjoy an all-day menu. For something a bit different they even offer private igloos that you can book, perfect for enjoying your own space or for a romantic occasion.

HARBOUR HOTEL BRIGHTON
64 Kings Road, BN1 1NA

With fantastic views of the beach, not only is Harbour Hotel perfectly dog friendly but it also boasts a luxurious subterranean spa. Each of the rooms exude an artistic air that reflects the local area with funky colours and art deco prints.

HILTON BRIGHTON METROPOLE
Kings Road, BN1 2FU

Perfectly located on the seafront, this grand Victorian hotel has all the city's main attractions on its doorstep. You'll find amazing views, gorgeously decked out rooms and dogs treated like guests themselves with beds, bowls and treats on arrival.

LOST IN THE LANES
10 Nile Street, BN1 1HW

Another gem hidden away in The Lanes, Lost in The Lanes is a quaint restaurant with contemporary food, which is most definitely Instagram worthy. It's renowned for its focus on fresh, locally sourced ingredients, and has an extensive menu from brunch to pastries. Dogs are welcome at the front of the restaurant.

OLIVE GROVE
15 Meeting House Lane, BN1 1HB

Set in The Lanes, Olive Grove is a Greek spin on tapas. It has a gorgeous outdoor courtyard area, complete with an olive tree, that makes you feel as though you have been transported to Europe. Of course, dogs are welcome inside and out, and the Olive Grove makes for a particularly great social meal if you are in a group.

EXPERIENCE FREEDOM GLAMPING
East Brighton Park, Wilson Avenue, BN2 5TS

Just outside the city, Experience Freedom Glamping is located in the South Downs National Park making it a peaceful retreat, while still being close to Brighton's vibrant centre. The site features safari tents, glamping pods and yurts to choose from, with dogs warmly welcomed and a range of walking routes right from the front door.

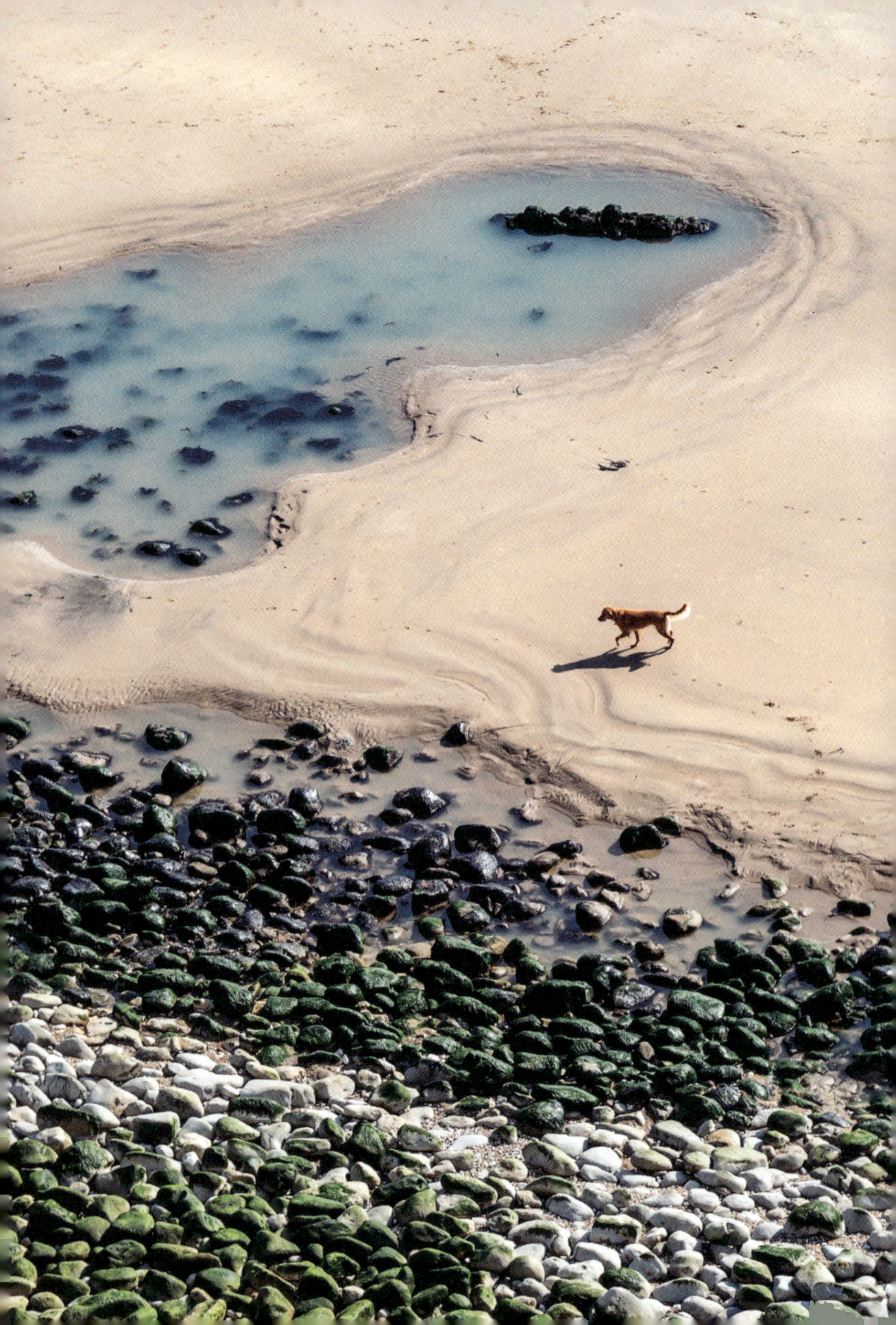

27.

Isle of Wight

Worth the boat ride, The Isle of Wight is a fantastic destination for dog-friendly holidays with expansive sandy beaches and coastal paths to woodland walks and historical landmarks to explore.

One of the island's highlights is Carisbrooke Castle, a historic fortress nestled in the heart of the island. Not only is it rich in history, but also incredibly welcoming to dogs. You can explore the castle grounds, including the beautiful medieval garden while your dog roams beside you on a lead. The surrounding rolling countryside offers wonderful views and if you're looking for a nearby walk, there are plenty leaving straight from the castle itself.

For something more unique, the Godshill Model Village is another must-see. The miniature recreation of the village of Godshill and Shanklin Old Village is a great way to whittle away a few hours, and one of few model villages that are dog friendly.

The surrounding village of Godshill itself is also not to be missed as it's one of the prettiest on the island, with thatched cottages, tea rooms and plenty of dog-friendly shops and cafés too.

The Isle of Wight Donkey Sanctuary is also great if you are an animal lover. You can wander the 55-acre sanctuary with your dog, meeting the friendly donkeys as you go and taking in the tranquil surrounding countryside.

Of course, the island also boasts a wide variety of dog-friendly walks. One of the most popular is the Tennyson Down walk, which takes you along towering chalk cliffs with breathtaking views of the English Channel. It's a circular 7-mile route which, while challenging, offers one of the best views of the iconic Needles on the island.

And there are plenty of dog-friendly beaches too, offering more relaxed routes, including Compton Bay and Yaverland Beach, which both have dog-friendly sections year-round. Compton Bay in particular is known for its fossil-rich cliffs, so be sure to keep an eye out as you stroll along the sands and wide-open spaces, which make it ideal for dogs to run freely.

Yaverland Beach is equally as stunning, with shallow waters that are ideal for paddling and sweeping views across the English Channel and nearby Culver Down providing a scenic backdrop.

Shanklin Chine is also a fantastic sight. A breathtaking natural gorge, it is renowned for its enchanting beauty and rich history. The deep tree-lined ravine has been shaped by centuries of water flow, which creates a magical atmosphere of cascading waterfalls, lush greenery and an abundance of wildlife. It's the sort of place where you'd expect fairies to live.

You can also walk to Shanklin Beach from here, a dog-friendly beach out of high season where dramatic cliffs meet the sea.

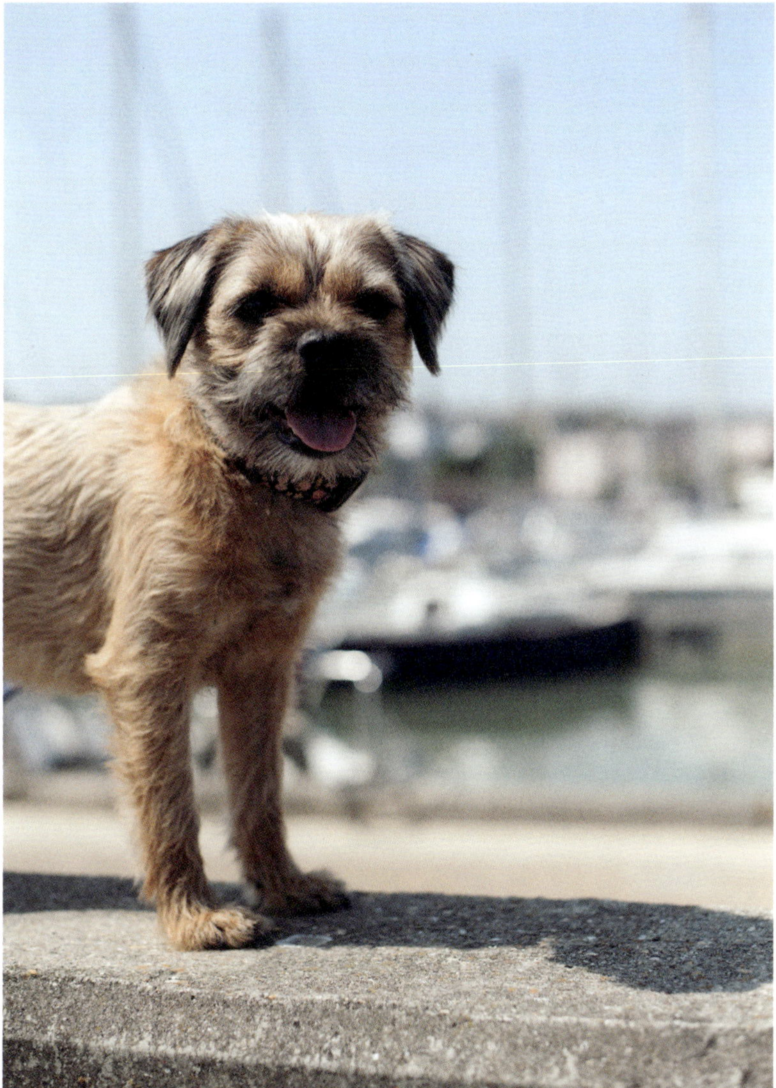

Places to explore

COMPTON BAY
Compton, PO30 4HB

An idyllic dog-friendly beach, Compton Bay is backed by dramatic chalk cliffs, and has a fantastic backdrop for leisurely walks along the shore to enjoy the natural beauty of the coastline.

GODSHILL MODEL VILLAGE
High Street, Godshill, Ventnor, PO38 3HH

Capturing the charm of a bygone era, Godshill Model Village features meticulously crafted replicas of the local area surrounded by beautifully landscaped gardens. It's a great place for a more relaxed day out, with dogs welcome on leads.

VENTNOR BOTANIC GARDEN
Undercliff Drive, Ventnor, IPO38 1UL

Surrounded by chalk downs, Ventnor Botanic Garden is home to an impressive collection of rare and exotic plant life. The unique microclimate here, which averages around 5 degrees warmer than the rest of the UK, means a variety of plants considered too tender for much of mainland Britain are able to thrive here alongside wildlife such as wall lizards and slow worms. There are expansive grounds to explore and dogs are welcome on leads.

SHANKLIN CHINE
Esplanade, Shanklin, PO37 6BW

A serene natural gorge, walk through a world fit for a fairytale with cascading waterfalls, ancient rock formations and enchanting woodlands. You'll find well-maintained footpaths that wind to its depth so you can fully appreciate its natural beauty.

Places to eat, drink and stay 🐾🐾

THE POINTER INN
High Street, Newchurch, Sandown, PO36 0NN

When you walk into a pub where everyone has a dog, you know it's bound to be somewhere where dogs are welcomed fondly. Such is the case with The Pointer Inn in Newchurch, one of the oldest and most historic pubs on the Isle of Wight. If the weather is good the beer garden is not to be missed, which leads on to a huge field where your dog can stretch their legs.

THE COW RESTAURANT AND BAR
Tapnell Farm, Newport Road, Yarmouth, PO41 0YJ

Housed in a converted swiss barn, The Cow must be on your list if you're looking for quality food. Situated at the heart of Tapnell Farm, this place is renowned for its delicious award-winning burgers. Dogs are welcome on the ground floor.

THE TAVERNERS
High Street, Godshill, Ventnor, PO38 3HZ

Brimming with history and character, The Taverners has everything you'd expect of a traditional seventeenth-century English pub. Oak beams, exposed stone walls, flagstone flooring and roaring open fireplaces make this a fantastic pit stop to warm up after an adventure exploring the local area.

WOODSIDE BAY LODGE RETREAT
Lower Woodside Road, Wootton Bridge, Ryde,
PO33 4JT

Set within a tranquil woodland you'll find comfortable and modern lodges that provide a perfect stay on the Isle of Wight. I love how they all have private decks, with amazing views, and some even come with hot tubs. There are also dog-friendly amenities on site, and walks through the woodland, plus there are a range of lodge sizes and types available to suit differing budgets.

THE ROYAL HOTEL
Belgrave Road, Ventnor, PO38 1JJ

Particularly perfect in the summer months, The Royal Hotel is a luxury option that boasts fantastic food and even its own outdoor pool, making you feel like you're in the South of France. Dogs can expect a luxurious experience here too, with dog bowls, treats, and even their own bottled water. On the doorstep you'll find the gorgeous hotel gardens, and a range of walking trails.

TAPNELL FARM HOLIDAY DESTINATION
Newport Road, Yarmouth, PO41 0YJ

Located in a beautiful rural setting, Tapnell Farm has a range of dog glamping options and cottages, including safari tents, cosy wood cabins and even geodesic domes which look like something out of a sci-fi film! The domes are a personal favourite, as you'll be able to perfectly enjoy the sunset and stargaze at night.

Bourton-on-the-Water

Broadway

Burford

Cotswolds

Bourton-on-the-Water   211

Burford   217

Broadway   225

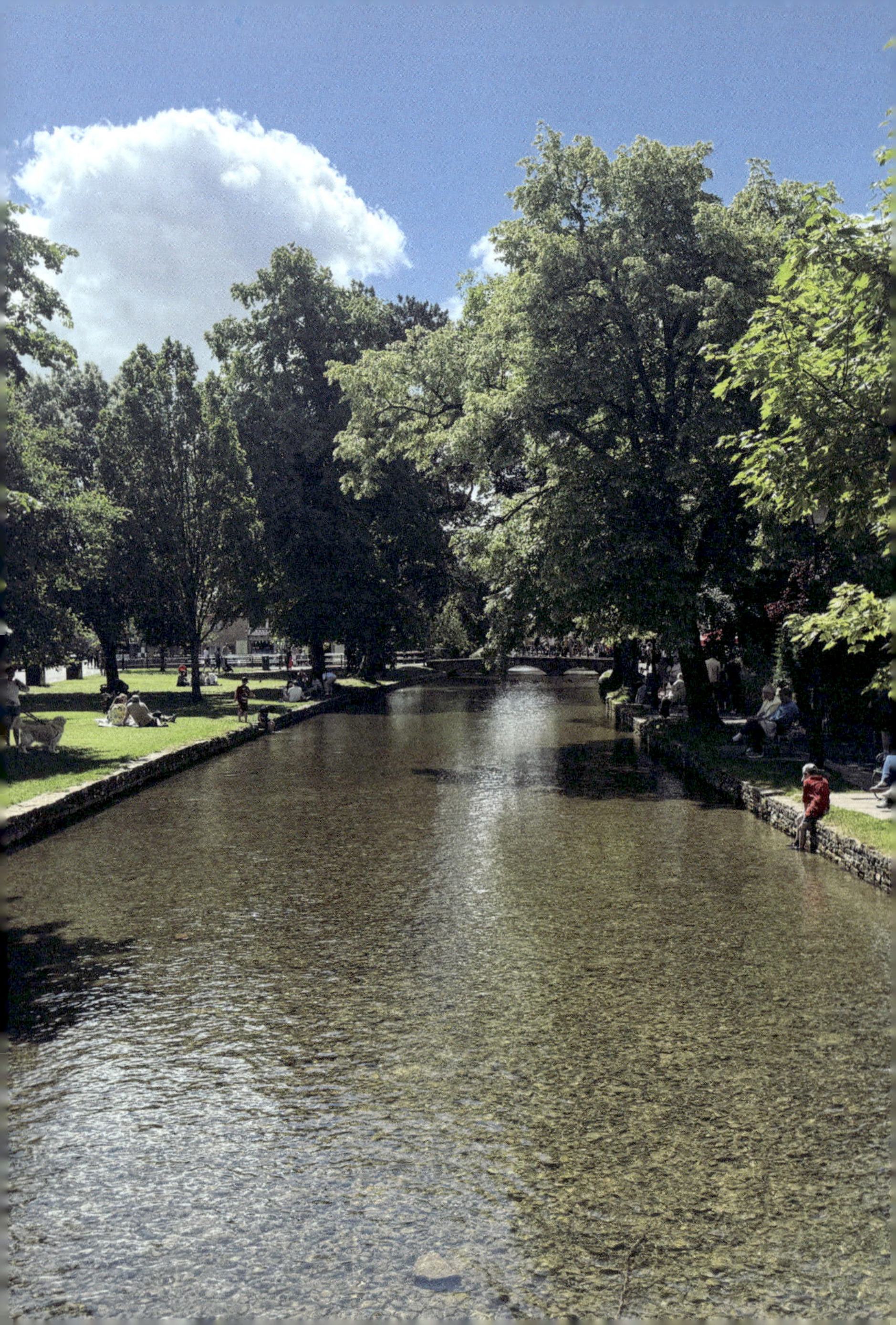

28.

Bourton-on-the-Water

Often referred to as the Venice of the Cotswolds, Bourton-on-the-Water exudes the exact type of village you think about when somebody says 'The Cotswolds'. It's home to 114 Grade II listed buildings and is regularly voted one of the prettiest villages in England.

No visit is complete without dipping a toe – or a paw – into the River Windrush. Shallow enough for safe paddling, the river runs directly through the heart of the village, creating the perfect spot for dogs to cool off on a warm day. Relax on the grass banks and enjoy a picnic or grab something to eat from one of the many dog-friendly cafés nearby. Make sure you pack a towel to dry your dog off!

A highlight is Birdland Park and Gardens, a dog-friendly wildlife park that's home to over 500 exotic and rare bird species including penguins, flamingos and pelicans. There are wide paths that meander around the park, which is surrounded by woodland and gardens, and often feeding demonstrations where you can learn more about the birds that live here.

For those with a keen interest in cars, the Cotswold Motoring Museum is also dog friendly. It's home to a vast collection of vintage cars, motorcycles, automobilia and is even the original home of childhood favourite, Brum.

Venturing just a short distance from Bourton-on-the-Water I would highly recommend the walk to the villages of Lower and Upper Slaughter where you'll get to experience what Cotswolds life is all about.

The villages are connected by a lovely riverside walk along the River Eye, which is particularly dog friendly. Both villages are picture-

perfect with honey-coloured stone cottages and ancient water mills. You won't want to forget your camera as the area is absolutely stunning.

If you're looking for more extensive walks, Bourton-on-the-Water provides access to several Cotswold walking trails, including The Windrush Way, a scenic 14-mile circular route linking Bourton-on-the-Water with Winchcombe and winding through rolling countryside, woods and open fields.

You'll find many access points to pick up the Cotswold Way, giving you and your dog chance to experience a section of this famous 102-mile national trail with spectacular views over the Severn Valley.

BIRDLAND PARK AND GARDENS

Rissington Road, GL54 2AY

Set within 9 acres of beautiful gardens and woodland, Birdland is home to over 500 exotic birds where your dog will get the opportunity to see anything and everything from pelicans to penguins. A must-visit if you're in the area, it's a great dog walk with a unique difference.

COTSWOLD MOTORING MUSEUM

The Old Mill, Sherbourne Street, GL54 2BY

Take a nostalgic journey through British motoring history in this Aladdin's cave of memorabilia. This is a great place to visit with kids and dogs as there are so many rooms to explore, including the home of Brum – the car from the iconic children's TV series. Dogs are welcome throughout.

THE OLD MILL

Mill Lane, Lower Slaughter, GL54 2HX

The most distinctive building in Lower Slaughter, The Old Mill is possibly one of the most photogenic spots in the whole of the Cotswolds. While the mill is sadly not dog friendly inside, it makes a fantastic starting point for a leisurely walk along the River Eye up to Upper Slaughter, which is equally as beautiful.

Places to eat, drink and stay 🐾🐾

THE PLOUGH INN
Chapel Lane, Cold Aston, GL54 3BN

A quaint village pub oozing with character that serves some of the best steak I've ever eaten. Inside, the pub is typical of a seventeenth-century inn, with flagstones, bare brick and low-beamed ceilings adding to the ambience of the place. It's no wonder it's a favourite among the locals.

OLD MANSE HOTEL
Victoria Street, GL54 2BX

Perfectly located overlooking the River Windrush, the Old Manse Hotel isn't short of historical charm and a warm and welcoming atmosphere. Built in the eighteenth century, it serves a variety of traditional British pub classics, and friendly staff ensure your dog feels right at home with water bowls and plenty of fuss.

THE COTTAGE AT ROBIN'S ROOST
Bobble Court, Little Rissington, GL54 2ND

Located in the sleepy hamlet of Little Rissington, The Cottage at Robin's Roost is just a short drive or walk away from Bourton-on-the-Water itself and surrounded by rolling countryside and scenic walks. Romantic and cosy, the cottage is the perfect base for exploring the local area.

THE COTSWOLD ANTIQUES AND TEA ROOM
2 Victoria Street, GL54 2BU

Full to the brim with collectables, antiques and retro items, at the back of this treasure trove of a shop you'll find a fantastic tea room where you can enjoy homemade cake, cream teas and more. Best of all they're dog friendly both inside and out.

THE STAG AT STOW
The Square, Market Square, Stow-on-the-Wold, GL54 1AF

A welcoming dog-friendly inn in the centre of nearby (and equally as beautiful) Stow-on-the-Wold, The Stag at Stow is completely dog friendly throughout. It's a beautifully restored Georgian townhouse, so you can expect elegance and character, with unique and individually decorated rooms.

GREYSTONES COTTAGE
Chapel Lane, Cold Aston, GL54 3BN

A 300-year-old Cotswold stone barn, Greystones Cottage is the perfect blend of comfort and countryside charm. A highlight is the secure garden, surrounded by beautiful pink roses in the summer, where dogs can play freely. Plus, it's next door to a dog-friendly pub – perfectly located if you ask me!

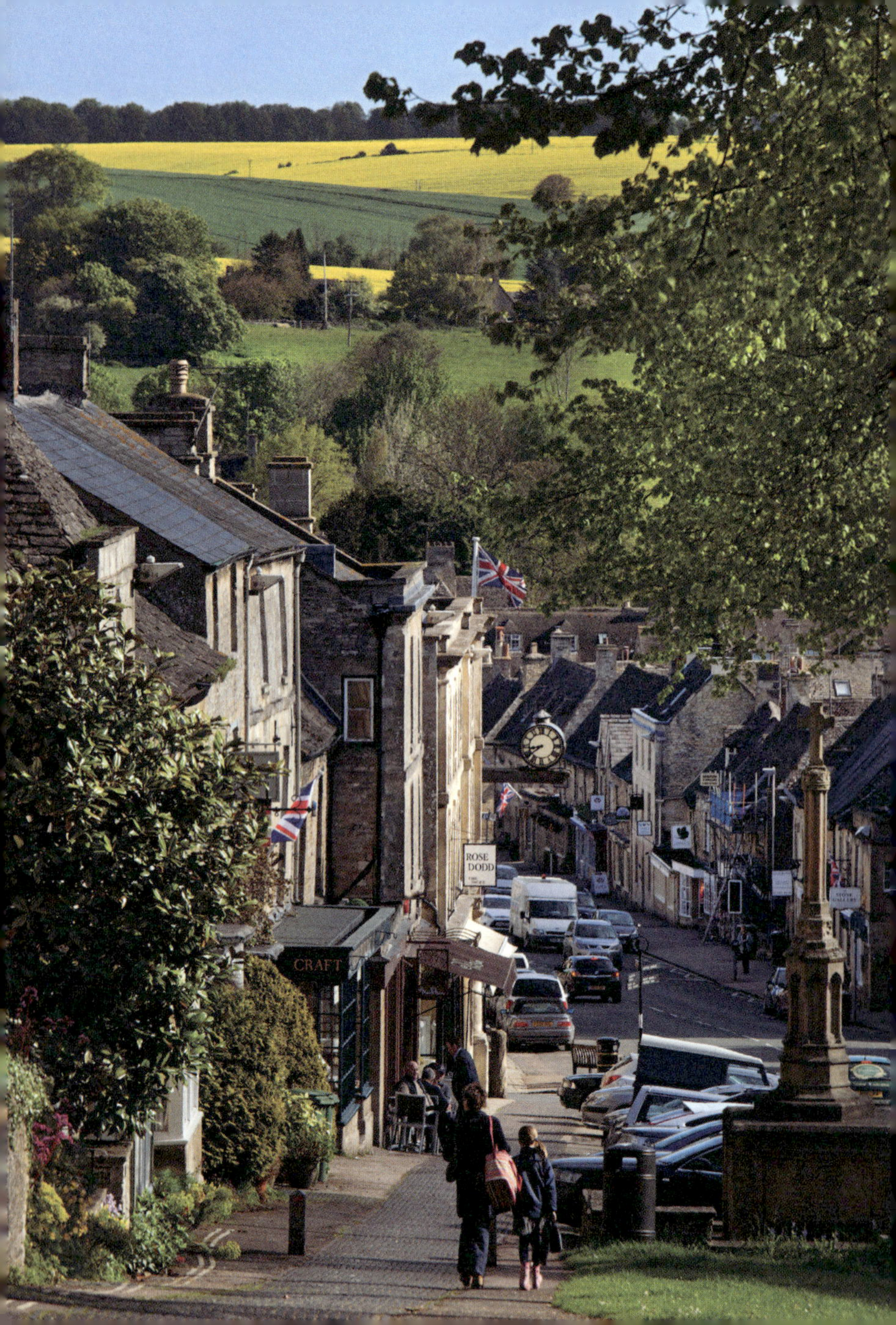
ROSE
DODD
CRAFT

29.

Burford

The perfect blend of ancient history and contemporary vibrancy, Burford is an idyllic town that captures the charm of this famous region.

The high street itself is lined with independent shops, quaint tearooms and historic pubs who welcome visitors and dogs with open arms, with many even providing water bowls and treats too.

A visit to Burford wouldn't be complete without a trip to Cotswold Wildlife Park and Gardens, one of the only dog-friendly wildlife parks in the UK. It's home to a diverse range of animals, from lions and giraffes to lemurs and monkeys, and dogs are welcome on leads across the majority of the park except for a few indoor enclosures. It's a fantastic doggy day out with a difference and your dog will definitely be worn out by the time you leave after all the excitement!

If you're interested in exploring more of the beautiful surrounding countryside, Burford is in a fantastic location to pick up several stunning walks. One popular route is the Windrush Valley Walk, which meanders along the river with scenic views of the Cotswold Hills, meadows and the ever-present charm of the historic architecture that is synonymous with the area. It's perfect for walking with dogs as it takes you through open countryside, tranquil woodland and quiet country lanes along gentle terrain.

A short drive from Burford lies the bustling market town of Chipping Norton, which is known for its quirky shops and vibrant art scene. There are numerous cafés and pubs where dogs are welcome, but it is also a great stopping point before heading to the nearby Rollright Stones, an ancient stone circle dating back over 4,000 years and steeped in history.

The stones form an atmospheric setting, which makes for a fantastic walk, rich with folklore and archaeological significance. It's also a wonderful opportunity to immerse yourself in the surrounding countryside with spectacular views of the Cotswold Hills on the distant horizon and wildflowers, including vibrant bluebells and delicate wild orchids peppering the landscape in the summer months.

For those who are fans of Clarkson's Farm, Diddly Squat Farm Shop is a fun addition to any day out. Located in the small village of Chadlington, the farm shop is a celebration of local produce, and you can even try out their famous 'cow juice' machine. There is also an outdoor area round the back where you can enjoy a drink and a snack.

The Cotswold Way is another fantastic route, which offers miles of trails winding through the area. One of my favourite routes starts in Great Barrington, a nearby village just a short drive from Burford, which passes stone cottages and lush meadows, and is especially scenic in autumn when the changing colours of the Cotswolds are at their most dramatic.

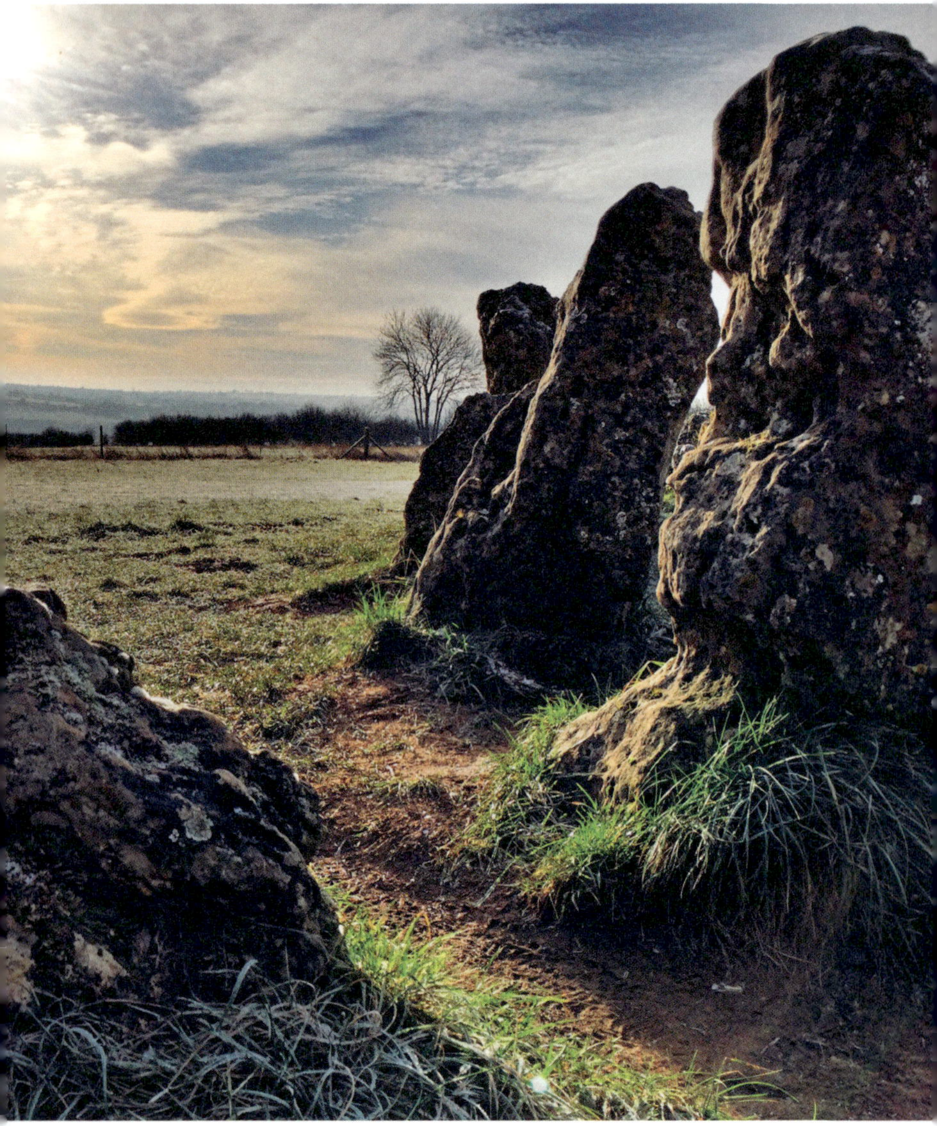

Places to explore

COTSWOLD WILDLIFE PARK AND GARDENS
Bradwell Grove, OX18 4JP

Possibly one of my favourite dog-friendly days out ever! Cotswold Wildlife Park is a fantastic destination for a day out with a difference. It's home to over 260 species of animals and allows dogs to accompany you on a lead throughout the majority of the grounds.

DIDDLY SQUAT FARM SHOP
5–12 Chipping Norton Road, Chadlington, OX7 3PE

Made famous by Jeremy Clarkson's hit TV series Clarkson's Farm, Diddly Squat Farm Shop is a must-visit for fans of the show. Just a few minutes out of Chipping Norton this quirky farm shop sells a selection of local produce, all with Clarkson's signature humorous twist. The shop is surrounded by farmland and even has a seating area at the back where you can grab a bite to eat and relax with your dog.

THE ROLLRIGHT STONES
Rollright Road, Little Rollright, OX7 5QB

A mysterious Neolithic stone circle steeped in legend and local history, the The Rollright Stones are an enchanting site that is a perfect spot for history buffs and nature lovers alike to explore with their dogs. I recommend taking a great walk that takes you here from Long Compton, approximately 4 miles in length so you can really appreciate the beauty of the place. Consider visiting in the golden hours of early morning or late evening when the sunlight casts long shadows across the landscape, enhancing the mystical aura of the stones.

Places to eat, drink and stay 🐾🐾

THE COTSWOLD ARMS
46 High Street, OX18 4QF

Located on Burford's historic high street, The Cotswold Arms is one of those family-run pubs that ticks all the boxes. Hearty and well-priced food, exceptionally friendly service, a cosy atmosphere, and dog treats and bowls on arrival – what more could you want!

THE FARMER'S DOG
Asthall Barrow Roundabout, OX18 4HJ

Another for lovers of Clarkson's Farm, the recently opened Farmer's Dog pub has a focus on local flavours and food. Whether you're a fan of Jeremy Clarkson or not, you'll find delicious food that showcases the best of British produce here, such as Cotswold-reared beef, seasonal veg and artisan cheeses from nearby dairies. As the name suggests the pub is very dog friendly.

THE KINGHAM PLOUGH
The Green, Kingham, OX7 6YD

A renowned dog-friendly pub, The Kingham Plough has a fantastic locally sourced and daily changing menu. If you're a foodie, you're not going to be disappointed. It's one of those places that doesn't just welcome dogs, but encourages it and you'll all be made to feel right at home.

BULL BURFORD
105 High Street, OX18 4RG

A traditional coaching inn, Bull Burford has a rustic and upmarket feel to it. The interiors are like nothing I've seen before, with dark colours providing a cosy feel and artwork at every turn. They have dedicated dog-friendly rooms, which are all located on the ground floor and have direct outdoor access, making it perfect for late-night toilet trips.

THE LAMB INN
Sheep Street, OX18 4LR

Quaint and full of atmosphere, The Lamb Inn is located just off the high street in Burford, giving you views of the picturesque town on one side and rolling countryside on the other. Originally a fifteenth-century weaver's cottage, it's definitely got that comfortable old-world charm to it. The rooms are all individually designed, with specific dog-friendly options available.

THE BAY TREE HOTEL
12 Sheep Street, OX18 4LW

Expect all the character of a Cotswolds inn, with big open fireplaces, exposed beams and flagstone floors. The Bay Tree Hotel is perfectly placed for exploring both Burford itself and the stunning countryside that lies just on its doorstep. What's more it's super dog friendly, and all four-legged guests receive a bed, bowl and even a sausage at breakfast.

30.

Broadway

Walking through Broadway feels like you've stepped onto the *Bridgerton* set. The high street, at the centre of the village, is one of the highlights – a broad tree-lined avenue with beautiful honey-coloured stone buildings.

Once an important stop on the coaching route from Worcester to London, the area remains a showcase of classic Cotswold architecture, from grand Georgian houses to charming, thatched cottages. Today the village is a vibrant blend of old and new, with the historic facades housing boutique shops, art galleries, antique stores and traditional tea rooms, many of which are dog friendly, all just waiting to be explored.

One of the first places that comes to mind when you think about Broadway is the Broadway Tower, the second highest point in the Cotswolds. The walk itself is gentle, but you'll find fantastic views of the surrounding area. Once you reach the top the iconic Broadway Tower stands proudly on the hill, making for a perfect photo opportunity, with panoramic views across the county. The surrounding area is also perfect for a picnic – I recommend heading into one of the delis in Broadway itself before your climb up.

If visiting in the summer months, Cotswold Lavender is also a must-see location. Located just outside the village, this family-run lavender farm becomes a sea of purple when the flowers are in full bloom and is an experience for all the senses. Dogs are welcome on leads and the spectacular backdrop means you are sure to get some Insta-worthy photos that you'll treasure for years to come. Make sure you try the lavender ice cream as it's delicious.

Broadway is also an excellent base for the walks that take in the area's natural beauty. Fish Hill Woods, located just outside the village is a stunning and peaceful walking route with a network of footpaths that wind through ancient woodland. There are a range of different routes you can take of varying length, and you can start the walk right from the village itself. It's a particular favourite of mine in the summer, as the cool shade from the towering trees provide a refreshing retreat.

Nearby you'll also find Batsford Arboretum, which is home to the country's largest private collection of trees and shrubs. It spans over

56 acres and is a feast for the senses in every season, with delicate blossoms in spring, peaceful greenery in summer and vivid reds and golds in autumn. It's a great spot for a leisurely walk and even has a dog-friendly café too.

In addition to its natural beauty and historic charm, Broadway is an ideal hub for exploring other parts of the Cotswolds. Snowshill is within easy reach and well known for its gorgeous location in the Cotswold Hills. It's another area that has surrounding landscape perfect for walking, with numerous routes right from the village.

Places to explore

COTSWOLD LAVENDER

Hill Barn Farm Cottage, Snowshill, WR12 7JY

Cotswold Lavender is a family-run farm that bursts into vibrant purple hues during the summer months. Typically, open from mid-June to early August, dogs are welcome throughout on leads. During these months the fields come alive and visitors are able to stroll along the vibrant rows of purple that stretch as far as the eye can see.

BROADWAY TOWER

Middle Hill, WR12 7LB

Perched atop one of the highest points in the Cotswolds, Broadway Tower is one of the best walks (and views) in the region. This iconic tower stands as a beacon among the beautiful surrounding landscape of open fields, wildflowers and woodlands, providing a home for local wildlife you might be lucky enough to spot such as hares, deer and birds of prey.

BATSFORD ARBORETUM AND GARDEN CENTRE

Batsford, Moreton-in-Marsh, GL56 9AT

On the outskirts of Moreton-in-Marsh, Batsford Arboretum is a dog-friendly haven with 56 acres of diverse woodland and tree collections to explore. Dogs on leads are welcome to explore the winding paths through stunning seasonal displays, which pass tranquil streams and ornamental pools. The dog-friendly café at the end of the walk ensures it ticks all the boxes for a great day out.

Places to eat, drink and stay 🐾🐾

TISANES TEAROOMS
Cotswold House, 21 The Green, WR12 7AA

If you're looking for a quintessentially British afternoon tea, Tisanes is the place to visit. Not only do they serve an extensive menu, its dog friendly inside and out too. The enclosed courtyard to the rear is particularly lovely in the summer months and a real hidden gem.

NUMBER 32
32 High Street, WR12 7DT

A relaxed café in the heart of Broadway, if you like good coffee this is the place to come. Perfect for breakfast or brunch, Number 32 serves the type of food that looks as good as it tastes with friendly staff who love dogs to boot.

COTSWOLD FARM PARK
Guiting Power, Cheltenham, GL54 5FL

Set on a working farm, Cotswold Farm Park has a range of accommodation such as lodges, pods and camping pitches, each offering comfort and picturesque country views. Surrounded by acres of farmland and nature trails, you won't be short of scenic walks to do here.

SNOWSHILL ARMS
Snowshill, WR12 7JU

Handily located halfway round a circular walk from Broadway, the Snowshill Arms makes for a fantastic stop-off to rest your legs and enjoy a drink or bite to eat. Inside, you'll find a cosy traditional pub feel with wooden beams, stone walls and a great selection of food, drink and beer, all surrounded by the sleepy village of Snowshill.

THE FISH HOTEL
Farncombe House, Campden Lane, WR12 7LH

The perfect country hotel, The Fish Hotel is set in a private 400-acre estate, meaning you'll have some amazing walkies right on your doorstep. On top of that, they even have a boot room, where you can borrow anything you might need from wellington boots to rain macs and even maps of local walks and a doggy shower.

THE LYGON ARMS
High Street, WR12 7DU

A properly dog-friendly hotel, The Lygon Arms has a range of dog-friendly rooms that all come with a bed, treats and bowls. They even have their very own dog menu in the restaurant where you can order a steak or chicken dinner! The hotel is right in the centre of Broadway, so you're never far away from all the action, surrounded by that quintessentially British feel that perfectly sums up the Cotswolds.

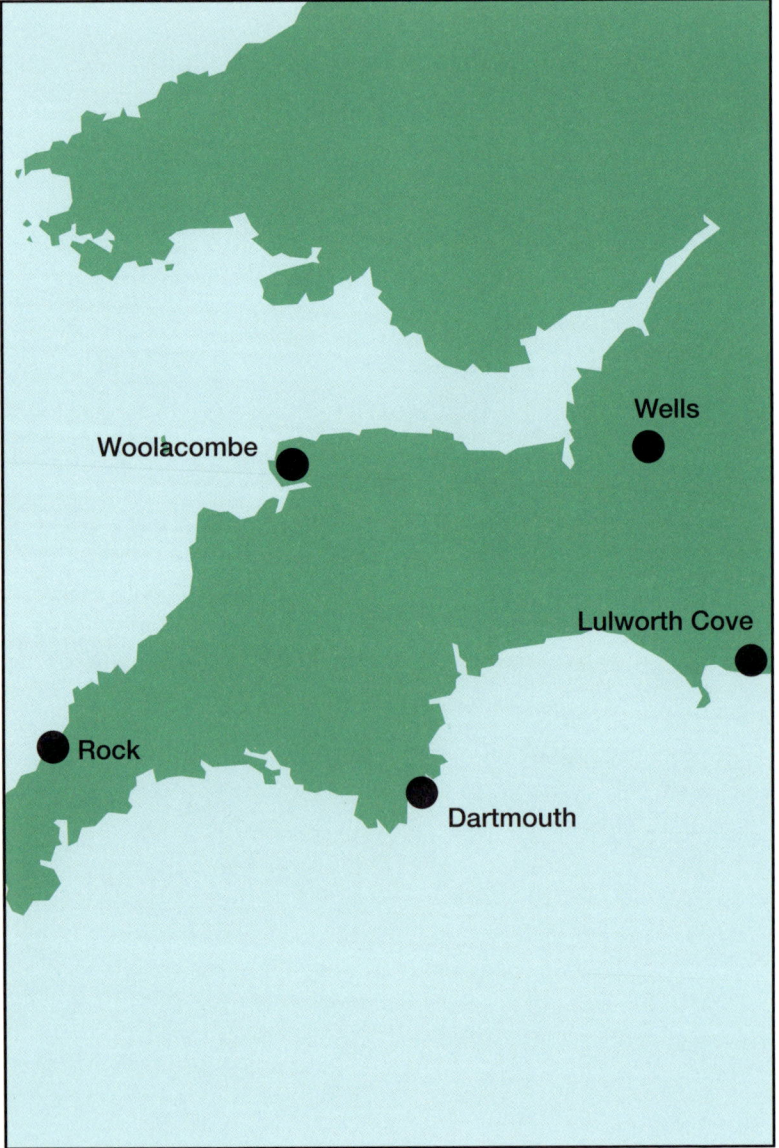

Woolacombe

Wells

Lulworth Cove

Rock

Dartmouth

South West

Dartmouth	235
Lulworth Cove	243
Wells	251
Rock	259
Woolacombe	265

31.

Dartmouth

Perched along the banks of the River Dart, Dartmouth is a beautiful and historic town, rich in maritime heritage and stunning coastal scenery. From the medieval streets to beautiful beaches, gorgeous countryside to a lush tree-lined river, this is not somewhere you'll be short of impressive adventures.

One of the town's best-kept secrets is Sugary Cove, a quiet and secluded beach at the mouth of the River Dart. Just a short walk from Dartmouth Castle, this hidden gem has crystal-clear blue waters where dogs can run freely year-round and splash in the shallow waters. Dramatic cliffs surround the cove and provide a scenic backdrop to this ideal spot to relax while listening to the rhythmic sounds of the waves.

Nearby Castle Cove is also worth exploring. Nestled beneath the imposing Dartmouth Castle it is another dog-friendly beach with gorgeous views across the river and out to sea. Dogs are also welcome in the castle grounds, where you can learn more about the town's rich history and spot seabirds soaring above.

For a longer walk, head to Strete Gate Beach, a more expansive shoreline along the South West Coast Path, and another beach where dogs are welcome all year round. Walk along to the adjoining Slapton Ley Nature Reserve and you'll be rewarded with a dog walking paradise. Home to rare and ellusive birds, such as Cetti's warbler and kingfisher, Slapton Ley Nature Reserve is the largest natural freshwater lake in the southwest. It's an amazing spot to enjoy the contrast between the lake and the wild ocean just a few steps away.

One of the best ways to experience Dartmouth's beauty is by boat, and dogs are welcome aboard many of the ferries that cross the River Dart. A favourite trip of mine is to Dittisham, a quaint village just upstream. The boat ride itself is full of sweeping views at every turn of the river's wooded banks, where you might even spot herons fishing. Once in Dittisham you can enjoy a walk along the water's edge, or consider heading over to Greenway, the former holiday home of famed author Agatha Christie.

The house, now managed by the National Trust, is set in an expansive woodland garden where a network of trails winds past ancient trees, colourful rhododendrons, and fragrant magnolias down to the riverbank. The landscape is truly enchanting, and the peaceful flow of the river and sounds of birdsong transport you to a world that inspired Christie's most famous works.

Places to explore

SLAPTON LEY NATIONAL NATURE RESERVE
Slapton, Kingsbridge, TQ7 2QP

The largest natural freshwater lake in southwest England, Slapton Ley is a haven for wildlife with its tranquil waters. Dogs are welcome to explore the various walking paths that wind through the reserve where you can admire the rich biodiversity, from the calls of Cetti's warblers hidden in the reeds to the graceful flight of marsh harriers above. Make sure you also head over to nearby Slapton Sands too, where you'll find miles of golden sand to run along.

GREENWAY
Greenway Road, Galmpton, Brixham, TQ5 0ES

The beloved holiday home of Agatha Christie, Greenway is a truly enchanting estate with expansive woodland gardens just waiting to be explored. Dogs are allowed to join you as you wander through this magical landscape, following trails that lead to peaceful riverbanks and secluded spots with breathtaking views of the River Dart.

DARTMOUTH CASTLE
Castle Road, Dartmouth, TQ6 0JN

Perched high on a cliff overlooking the mouth of the River Dart, Dartmouth Castle boasts impressive views and a historic charm. The castle's walls and turrets create a dramatic backdrop as you meander through the grounds taking in the fresh sea breeze and stunning views of the coastline.

Places to eat, drink and stay 🐾🐾

FERRY BOAT INN
Manor Street, Dittisham, TQ6 0EX

This quirky pub with fantastic views of the river is everything you'd expect from a small village establishment – friendly staff, locals round the bar and super welcoming to families and dogs alike. Inside there is a cosy atmosphere with low ceilings and traditional décor – make sure you sit by the window if there are seats available; it's one of the most gorgeous scenes you'll see from a pub window where you can sit and watch boats come and go down the peaceful River Dart.

LEONARDS COVE HOLIDAY VILLAGE
New Road, Stoke Fleming, TQ6 0NR

Perched on the clifftops overlooking the stunning south Devon coast, Leonards Cove Holiday Park is a peaceful retreat just moments away from Dartmouth and the golden sands of Blackpool Sands beach. There are a range of accommodation options here to cater to all preferences, from cosy self-catering lodges and charming cottages to a well-equipped campsite. They have a range of dog-friendly options.

ROCKFISH

8 South Embankment, TQ6 9BH

With a no-nonsense menu, Rockfish is an upmarket fish 'n' chip restaurant that retains that classically British feel and serves some of the freshest fish I've ever tasted. That's probably because the seafood here is served fresh from what's been landed by the fleet in nearby Brixham that morning. Delicious! Dogs are welcome inside and out.

THE RIVER SHACK

The Quay, Stoke Gabriel, Totnes, TQ9 6RD

With a laid-back vibe, The River Shack café boasts some of the best views of the River Dart. There is a gorgeous terrace right on the waterside and dogs are also allowed inside too. You can expect some fantastic fresh seafood dishes here, with menus that change regularly to reflect the seasons.

BAYARDS COVE INN

27 Lower Street, TQ6 9AN

Situated on Dartmouth's cobbled quayside, this timber-framed Tudor inn stands proud at the harbour entrance and couldn't be better located. You'll be right on the South West Coast path, and friendly staff are always happy to recommend one of the many routes you can take from the doorstep. Dogs are treated like guests in their own right here with dog beds, bowls and locally made treats on arrival.

DITTISHAM HIDEAWAY – TREEHOUSES, SHEPHERDS LODGES AND AMERICAN AIRSTREAM

Dittisham, TQ6 0JB

If you're looking for the perfect relaxing escape, Dittisham Hideaway ticks all the boxes. It's set in the heart of the Devon countryside in a secluded valley with a bubbling stream. They have a range of luxury treehouses (don't worry, no climbing required!), an airstream trailer and gorgeous shepherd's huts, all of which are dog friendly. Dogs are greeted with a dog bed, water, food bowls, treats, toys and even a welcome letter.

32.

Lulworth Cove

Positioned along Dorset's Jurassic Coast, Lulworth Cove offers one of the most breathtaking and dog-friendly walking adventures in the UK. The bay at the base of the village is a natural amphitheatre, sculpted by thousands of years of coastal erosion and is an awe-inspiring adventure and starting point to many fantastic walks.

Just a short walk from Lulworth Cove is the famous Durdle Door. This limestone arch is one of the most photographed landmarks in the UK, and it's easy to see why as it rises majestically from the sea. The trail from Lulworth hugs the cliff's edge as you walk up from the village and eventually leads down to the shingle beach below, which is dog friendly year-round. If you're up for an early start, head here at sunrise for some truly awe-inspiring scenes and photos, and to beat the crowds, I promise it will be worth it.

Venturing further inland, I also recommend heading to the abandoned village of Tyneham, which offers a poignant glimpse into history. Evacuated during World War II and never repopulated, Tyneham is now a ghost village preserved in time. As you wander through the deserted streets it's easy to imagine the lives once lived here.

From here you can take a short walk down to Worbarrow Bay, winding down paths through the rolling countryside. The final stretch of the walk descends towards the secluded but vast cove, which is another dog-friendly beach year-round. Unlike the busier beaches further along the coast, Worbarrow Bay feels like a hidden gem, a quiet retreat where your dog can explore the shingle beach and paddle in the clear waters.

Another must-visit is Studland Bay, a dog-friendly paradise that to me looks as though it could be the French Riviera on a warm summer's day. This unspoilt gem has a dog-friendly section year-round, and the shallow waters make it perfect for swimming. Bordered by heathland and part of a national nature reserve, it's also rich in wildlife. Ospreys are known to visit during their migration, and the bay is an important habitat for seabirds.

The walk here to Studland Bay is another fantastic route to add to your list. The coast path takes you across the dramatic cliffs offering panoramic views of the shoreline below. On a clear day you'll even be able to see across to the Isle of Purbeck and even the Isle of Wight. As you ascend, you'll soon reach Old Harry Rocks, towering chalk formations that rise dramatically from the sea, their brilliant white rock contrasting with the deep blue of the sea below.

Once in Swanage, unwind at one of the many dog-friendly restaurants or cafés before exploring the town and either enjoying the walk back, or hopping on the bus that runs direct to Studland.

Places to explore

DURDLE DOOR
West Lulworth, BH20 5PU

Have you even visited the Jurassic Coast if you've not been to Durdle Door? Known for its magnificent natural limestone arch that dramatically juts out into the sea, this spectacular rock formation has been formed by millions of years of coastal erosion and is a must-visit for anyone exploring the area. The pebble beach is dog friendly year-round, and the clear turquoise waters make it perfect for a paddle. For a quieter option head to Man O'War Beach next door, which is equally as stunning.

TYNEHAM VILLAGE
Wareham, BH20 5DE

The village where time stood still in 1943. Evacuated in World War II, this village is a fantastic glimpse into life of the past and makes for a peaceful walk as you wander around the deserted cottages, church and even a schoolhouse.

STUDLAND BAY
Knoll Beach, Hardys Road, Studland, BH19 3AH

A dog-friendly haven, this expansive stretch of golden sand bordered by rolling dunes and heathland is the perfect playground for dogs and humans alike. The beach has shallow, gentle waters, which are perfect for doggy paddles, while the surrounding rugged terrain is home to several fantastic walks.

Places to eat, drink and stay

LULWORTH COVE INN
Main Road, BH20 5RQ

Located just up from the beach, Lulworth Cove Inn couldn't be better placed for relaxing after a walk along the coast. This historic inn has a contemporary feel with local fossils and art dotted around the place, and you'll find it's always bustling inside. There is an extensive menu with daily specials and dogs are welcomed.

THE BOAT SHED CAFÉ
Lulworth Cove, B20 5RQ

Oozing coastal charm, The Boat Shed Café has a fantastic view and is beautifully informal. There is a very welcoming atmosphere here and no fuss – the perfect place to soak up the surrounding landscape. There's not much better than enjoying a bacon sandwich or a traditional cream tea here. Dogs are welcome inside and out.

THE DOLLS HOUSE
Main Road, West BH20 5RQ

A traditional sweet shop and tea garden, The Dolls House is particularly lovely in the summer, where you can enjoy delicious ice cream in the surrounding garden that is filled with flowers. Inside, be sure to pick up some of the luxurious fudge or original sweets to give you a sugar boost while out on a walk.

DURDLE DOOR HOLIDAY PARK
Main Road, BH20 5PU

The closest you can stay to Durdle Door, this holiday park is surrounded by an unspoilt rural landscape and stunning coastline. Dogs are welcome in the range of accommodation options from holiday homes and glamping pods, to skylight cabins and basic camping pitches. They even have a dog-friendly bar and restaurant on site, which is super dog friendly, complete with dog treats.

BISHOPS COTTAGE
Main Road, BH20 5RQ

Bishops Cottage is a beautiful guest house just a stone's throw from the coast. There's even an outdoor swimming pool and beautiful gardens on top of the cliff that overlooks Lulworth Cove – perfect for enjoying some quiet away from the crowds. It's dog friendly and welcomes dogs regardless of shape or size.

THE SHELTER SHED
Durdle Door Holiday Cottages, BH20 5PU

Located on the Lulworth Estate, The Shelter Shed is a cosy barn, which would make a great romantic break for two. Part of a complex of several other cottages there is also access to a heated outdoor swimming pool and games room – perfect for winding down after long walks on the coast. And it's fantastically dog friendly, with bowls and towels all provided, plus a great welcome pack for humans too.

33.

Wells

Picturesque streets, historic buildings and miles of surrounding natural beauty, Wells is a charming city in Somerset with an amazing array of dog-friendly adventures and a great destination to visit.

Situated on the edge of the Mendip Hills, Wells is one of England's smallest cities, and dominated by the impressive Wells Cathedral. A spectacular example of Gothic architecture the towering spires and delicate carved figures make it an awe-inspiring place to visit. Dogs are surprisingly allowed both inside and out on a lead, so you can both enjoy the wow-factor this stunning place brings and soak up the history of the place before heading for a stroll among the serene Cloister Gardens.

Wells itself is filled with enchanting narrow streets lined with historic buildings and cosy shops, and you can easily while away several hours exploring the city's timeless appeal.

There are also some fantastic walks right from the city itself, with the walk to Dulcote and Dinder a particularly great opportunity to experience the local countryside. The 4.5-mile route is perfect for a leisurely stroll and particularly scenic as it winds around the Bishop's Palace.

Nearby the dramatic cliffs and rugged beauty of Cheddar Gorge provide a more challenging adventure. The gorge is renowned for its impressive rock formations and deep chasms, which have been carved by glacial meltwater over millennia.

As you traverse the gorge there is a network of well-marked walking routes that reveal an array of stunning viewpoints and geological marvels. The main route, known as the Gorge Walk, follows the winding path alongside the cliffs and provides spectacular views. Be sure to keep your furry friend close and on a lead as you navigate the more rugged terrain.

En route, make sure you stop off at Gorgeous Animals, a dedicated doggy bakery, yes you read that right, where you'll find doggy birthday cakes, doughnuts, biscuits and even ice cream.

Ebbor Gorge Nature Reserve is another magical walking route, surrounded by lush woodland, hidden caves and views across the Somerset Levels. Similarly to Cheddar, Ebbor Gorge is renowned for its dramatic landscape characterised by deep winding gorges. There are a variety of routes throughout the reserve where a dense canopy of trees filters dappled sunlight onto the forest floor, and vibrant carpets of bluebells appear in spring months.

For something a little different, head to Glastonbury, which isn't far from Wells and is often associated with King Arthur, the Holy Grail and even witchcraft and magic. The walk up the Tor is well worth the climb, and you'll be rewarded with panoramic views of the surrounding countryside.

Places to explore

GLASTONBURY TOR

Chilkwell Street, Glastonbury, BA6 8DB

An iconic hill rising majestically from the Somerset landscape, Glastonbury Tor is a beacon of both historical significance and natural beauty. The ascent to the Tor is a gorgeous route, beginning with a gentle climb through lush meadows and past ancient hedgerows before breaking out to reveal a sweeping panorama of the landscape below, including views stretching as far as the Mendip Hills and the Somerset Levels. Parking is available at Chilkwell Street, where you can take a short route from the town to the summit.

CHEDDAR GORGE AND CAVES

The Cliffs, Cheddar, BS27 3QF

A spectacular limestone ravine, Cheddar Gorge is one of the most dramatic and awe-inspiring landscapes in Somerset. The gorge's towering cliffs soar up to 137 metres high creating a breathtaking backdrop of rugged rock formations and setting the scene for stunning walks across winding trails.

WELLS CATHEDRAL

Cathedral Green, Wells, BA5 2UE

A masterpiece standing proud in the centre of the city, Wells Cathedral is an incredible example of Gothic architecture that takes you back to the medieval era with intricate stone carvings and an awe-inspiring facade that has stood the test of time. The cathedral is actually dog-friendly inside and out, with the lush historic grounds providing ample space to explore and appreciate the cathedral's grandeur from every angle.

Places to eat, drink and stay 🐾🐾

THE BISHOP'S TABLE
The Bishop's Palace and Gardens, Market Place, BA5 2PD

Set in the beautiful gardens of The Bishop's Palace, The Bishop's Table serves locally sourced food and some of the best cakes in Wells. It has fantastic views over the croquet lawn and Palace buildings. Dogs are welcome inside and out.

THE ANCIENT GATEHOUSE HOTEL
20 Sadler Street, BA5 2SE

If you're looking for a stay with views of the Cathedral look no further. The Ancient Gatehouse is just yards away from the market place in the medieval heart of the city. It's a small bed and breakfast, with rooms retaining its original features, some even boasting a four-poster bed. Dogs are welcome throughout.

THE CROSSWAYS
Stocks Lane, North Wootton, BA4 4EU

Located a short distance from both Wells and Glastonbury in the heart of Somerset, The Crossways is a luxury 5-star accommodation with each room boasting bags of character. The hotel has glorious views over towards Glastonbury Tor, and dogs are welcome in all areas except the restaurant.

THE CROWN AT WELLS
Market Place, BA5 2RP

Dating back to the fifteenth century, the Crown is as dog friendly as it gets, with staff that truly love dogs. The pub is quaint and traditional, and looks out onto the heart of Wells Market Place. The Sunday roasts are truly something special, particularly nice to chow down on in the autumn and winter months as you cosy up with your dog next to the roaring open fire.

LION ROCK TEA ROOMS
The Cliffs, Cheddar, BS27 3QE

Nestled in the heart of Cheddar Gorge, you can't miss this gorgeous blue building that hides beneath the famous Lion Rock. It's worth coming just to gasp at the beauty of the place. Inside is everything you would expect from a traditional British tearoom, with afternoon teas and cakes galore. If it's sunny, try for a table outside so you can truly soak up the setting. Dogs are welcomed here, and it has a great reputation for being friendly and inviting.

STRAWBERRYFIELD PARK LUXURY LODGES
Draycott, Cheddar, BS27 3FN

A gorgeous selection of self-catering lodges, Strawberryfield is perfectly located between Cheddar and Wells with stunning views over the Somerset Levels. They have a range of dog-friendly accommodation options, all of which are beautifully decorated and boast their own private hot tub.

34.

Rock

On the Camel Estuary's northern shores you'll find Rock, a dog-friendly gem in Cornwall. Often referred to as the 'Kensington of Cornwall', it is rich in serene beauty and appeal as a getaway destination and offers a peaceful retreat from busier Cornish towns.

Unlike a lot of beaches in Cornwall, Rock Beach and the surrounding beaches here are dog-friendly year-round, which boosts its appeal. Rock's golden sands stretch wide at low tide, creating a peaceful haven for dogs to run and explore.

One of the highlights of visiting Rock, is the opportunity to take the passenger ferry across to Padstow. The short boat ride, which welcomes dogs on board, is a unique way to travel and the views across the estuary are stunning. Your dog will relish the opportunity to feel the sea breeze on their face as you cruise across the bay.

Once you arrive in Padstow, you'll find a lively town that is equally as welcoming to dogs, with many cafés and pubs offering dog-friendly seating. You can spend the whole day here wandering through the town's cobbled lanes past an array of pastel-coloured cottages, traditional Cornish pubs and boutique shops and galleries.

The scent of freshly caught seafood fills the air in the bustling harbour, where you can grab fish

and chips and enjoy watching the fishing boats come and go among the estuary and surrounding hills.

Further along the coast, Daymer Bay is another dog-friendly beach that's ideal for a visit. It sits just around the corner from Rock and is accessible by either a short drive, or a pleasant coastal walk. The soft sandy beach here is sheltered and peaceful, not to mention perfect for dogs who love to swim, as the waters are calm and shallow. The scenery here is quintessentially Cornish, with the coastline stretching out and the horizon meeting the sea in a seamless blend of blue and green.

One of the most scenic routes you can do here is taking the South West Coast Path from Rock all the way past Daymer Bay and on to Polzeath. The coast path follows the breathtaking coastline and it really is one of the most beautiful coastal walks with beaches, stunning headlands and gorgeous vistas of the glistening Atlantic Ocean.

The walk combines natural beauty with history, as you can visit the grave of the famous poet John Betjeman, who is buried at St Enodoc Church, tucked away in the sand dunes near Daymer Bay.

Another enjoyable walk is the circular route you can take from Rock all the way to Porthilly Beach. It's less busy than some of the more popular routes, making it ideal if you are looking for a quieter experience with your dog. The route takes you along the estuary, where you can watch the tides ebb and flow, transforming the landscape throughout the day.

Places to explore

ROCK – PADSTOW PASSENGER FERRY

Ferry Slip, Rock, Wadebridge, PL27 6LD

This short but picturesque boat ride is a must-do when visiting the area and provides a quick way to visit the nearby fishing town of Padstow. Here, you'll be able to explore Padstow's narrow, winding streets, quaint boutiques and cafés, and waterfront paths. The ferry runs regularly throughout the day making it a convenient and enjoyable way to experience both Rock and Padstow with your dog.

DAYMER BAY

Wadebridge, PL27 6SA

Tucked between Rock and Polzeath, this fantastic dog-friendly beach is the perfect blend of golden sands, calm waters and unspoilt beauty. The sheltered bay is a haven for dogs, who can explore its wide, open spaces year-round without any restrictions. Plus, the gentle shallow waters make it the perfect place for dogs to swim, while the surrounding dunes and grassy headlands provide excellent walking paths.

POLZEATH BEACH

Wadebridge, PL27 6TB

One of my favourite beaches in Cornwall, I have such happy memories here as a child. The beach is framed by dramatic cliffs and rocky outcrops, offering spectacular coastal scenery and a variety of beautiful walking routes along the South West Coast Path. Dogs are welcome here during the off-season, and in summer out of peak hours. However, it's still worth visiting even in the height of summer, as you can explore the local paths taking in the gorgeous views and spotting surfers dart in among the waves.

Places to eat, drink and stay 🐾🐾

🍽️ THE UPPER DECK
5 Beachside, Rock Road, PL27 6FD

The Upper Deck is a relaxed restaurant that embodies the chilled essence of Cornwall. Expect laid-back vibes with a fantastic view over the estuary. It's super dog friendly here, and if it's sunny you'll definitely want to sit on the terrace!

🍽️ PRAWN ON THE LAWN
Padstow, 11 Duke Street, Padstow, PL28 8AB

Being a fishing town, Padstow is full of great seafood restaurants, but none quite compare to Prawn on the Lawn. They serve seafood with a difference, combining inventive and delicate flavours. Space is tight, so make sure you book ahead and let them know you'll be bringing your furry friend along too.

🍽️ TJ'S SURF CAFÉ, ROOF TERRACE & BAR
Dunders Hill, Polzeath, Wadebridge, PL27 6TB

This perfect beachside surf café provides stunning vistas over Polzeath Beach. It serves simple but delicious food, and even a special doggy menu. It does get busy, so booking is recommended particularly in the summer months.

HARBOUR HOTEL PADSTOW
Station Road, Padstow, PL28 8DB

Located in a prime position for exploring Padstow, this dog-friendly Victorian boutique hotel boasts fantastic views across the Camel Estuary towards Rock. There are nine dog friendly rooms, with bowls and treats on arrival, and humans will be delighted too as they are welcomed by a decanter of gin and luxury toiletries.

BODMIN JAIL HOTEL
Scarlett's Well Road, Bodmin, PL31 2PL

Around 15 miles away from Rock you'll find Bodmin Jail Hotel, a stay with a massive quirky difference! A former prison, it has been transformed into a four-star hotel. Each room has an equal abundance of history, with original cell doors and other authentic features alongside the luxury you'd expect, such as freestanding baths and walk-in showers. Dogs won't miss out on the luxury either, with a comfy bed, water bowl and tasty treats provided.

HIGHCLIFFE CORNWALL
Francis Lane, Trebetherick, PL27 6TS

Just moments from the coast path, Highcliffe has a range of stylish dog-friendly holiday homes that are perfectly located for exploring the local scenery. They all have a reverse living concept, so the living rooms allow you to gaze out across the exquisite coastal views. All of the properties are dog friendly and have up to four bedrooms, so are great for larger family groups.

35.

Woolacombe

Famous for its expansive golden beach that stretches as far as the eye can see, Woolacombe is snuggled between dramatic headlands, rolling hills and stretches of unspoilt countryside.

The crown jewel is its award-winning beach, a 3-mile stretch of fine sand that has been recognised as one of the best beaches in the UK, and it's easy to see why. Woolacombe Beach has a large, designated dog-friendly area, so they'll be able to run across the sand while the sound of crashing waves and the refreshing ocean breeze set the tone for a peaceful seaside adventure.

If you're looking for a more secluded beach experience, a short drive north will take you to Lee Bay, a quiet cove surrounded by lush green cliffs. This hidden gem is dog friendly and perfect for a peaceful walk, especially at low tide when the beach opens up to reveal rock pools and secluded spots ideal for exploring.

There are lots of fantastic walks from here too, one of the most popular routes takes you along the South West Coast Path. Heading east from the beach, you can venture towards Morte Point, a stunning headland with panoramic views across to Lundy Island. The route is filled with dramatic coastal landscapes, jagged rocks and steep cliffs, and if you're lucky you might spot seals basking in the sun.

Another highlight on the coast path is Baggy Point, a gentle circular walk with views stretching across the bay and beyond. The route leads through fields and along cliff edges, where you might even spot dolphins playing in the surf below and seabirds nesting on the cliffs. It's a particularly fantastic spot for nature lovers and photographers, with its dramatic coastal panoramas and rich biodiversity.

For a more leisurely stroll, head to the grassy dunes of Woolacombe Warren. These rolling sand dunes are a designated Site of Special Scientific Interest (SSSI), home to rare plants and wildlife. As you meander through the warren you'll find a network of trails that weave through the dunes, offering views across the beach and out to sea. It makes the ideal walk for dogs who will love the freedom to roam among the grasslands and sandy paths.

Not only great for walks, Woolacombe is also known for its surf-friendly waves. Some local surf schools, like Woolacombe Surf Centre, offer dog-friendly paddleboarding sessions, so if you're both brave enough you can take your dog out on the water with you!

Alternatively, if you'd prefer to stay dry, boat trips from nearby Ilfracombe are a great option with many allowing dogs on board. As you set sail from the harbour, the rugged cliffs rise majestically from the sea, and the trips often provide the chance to spot dolphins, seals, and even the occasional basking shark gliding through the waters.

Places to explore

WOOLACOMBE BAY

Barton Road, EX34 7DF

A glorious 3-mile stretch of golden sand, Woolacombe is renowned for its beauty and being dog friendly year-round. With its wide-open expanse and gently sloping shores, it's a fantastic spot for long walks with your dog, especially at low tide when the beach seems endless.

ILFRACOMBE SEA SAFARI

Harbour the pier, Ilfracombe, EX34 9EQ

For a thrilling adventure on the water, Ilfracombe Sea Safari has several dog-friendly cruises setting off from the picturesque harbour. The tour takes you along North Devon's rugged coastline, exploring dramatic cliffs, hidden coves and diverse wildlife. Keep an eye out for seals, dolphins and even the occasional porpoise as you cruise through some of the UK's most striking coastal scenery.

MORTE POINT

Mortehoe near Woolacombe, EX34 7DT

Morte Point is a gorgeous headland offering some of the most spectacular coastal views in North Devon. Managed by the National Trust, this rugged dog-friendly location is known for its jagged rocks, rolling hills and breathtaking views. The coastal path here is a walker's dream, with opportunities to spot seals basking on the rocks. To access the route, I recommend parking at the National Trust Mortehoe Car Park where you can follow the trail to the headland.

Places to eat, drink and stay 🐾🐾

THE DOLPHIN
7 The Quay, Ilfracombe, EX34 9EQ

For a true taste of the British seaside, The Dolphin is the perfect spot to grab classic fish and chips, served with an unbeatable view of the bustling quay. Perched right by the water, dogs are welcome inside, although I'd recommend grabbing your food to go and eating on the harbour as you take in the coastal views.

FLAME FACTORY
9 The Quay, Appledore, Bideford, EX39 1QS

Located in the village of Appledore just a scenic drive from Woolacombe, Flame Factory is known for its inventive and delicious wood-fired pizzas. The menu offers everything from classic toppings to more unique options like pulled pork and pear. Dogs are warmly welcomed throughout.

WOOLACOMBE BAY HOLIDAY PARK
Sandy Lane, EX34 7AH

Perched up on a hill overlooking the bay, you can see the beach from almost anywhere on this picturesque caravan park. In fact, you'll only be 15 minutes' walk away from the huge sandy Woolacombe Bay. There's a range of different accommodation options here and dogs are welcome across the park.

WOOLACOMBE BEACH RETREATS
South Street, EX34 7BY

A range of dog-friendly accommodation, Woolacombe Beach Retreats cluster of coastal homes has everything you need to feel at home. Each property blends comfort with coastal charm, featuring stylish interiors where you and your dog can unwind after a day of beachside adventures.

BEACH HOUSE BAR AND RESTAURANT
Granville Terrace, 3 West Road, EX34 7BW

A coastal gem where seafood takes centre stage, this restaurant perfectly captures the essence of the ocean. Each dish is crafted with subtle flavouring to let the natural tastes of the sea truly shine. The restaurant has a bright and airy interior, and its relaxed, beachy vibe makes it a welcoming space for both humans and dogs alike.

CROFT APARTMENT
Pool Lane, Mortehoe, EX34 7EJ

Situated on the edge of Woolacombe, this single storey apartment is ideally located for exploring the South West Coast Path. It's a little off the beaten track, but perfect if you'd like to escape to the serene countryside. There's a gorgeous private balcony where you can soak up the fresh sea air and savour the tranquillity of the North Devon coast, while inside there's a light and airy vibe.